GODFORSAKEN

THE CROSS –
THE GREATEST HOPE OF ALL

A Book for Lent and Holy Week

STEPHEN COTTRELL

HODDER &
STOUGHTON

First published in Great Britain in 2022 by Hodder & Stoughton
An Hachette UK company

1

A CIP catalogue record for this title is available from the British Library

Hardback ISBN 978 1 399 80524 7
eBook ISBN 978 1 399 80526 1

Typeset in Sabon MT by Palimpsest Book Production Ltd, Falkirk, Stirlingshire

Printed and bound in Great Britain by Clays Ltd, Elcograf S.p.A.

Hodder & Stoughton policy is to use papers that are natural, renewable
and recyclable products and made from wood grown in sustainable forests.
The logging and manufacturing processes are expected to conform
to the environmental regulations of the country of origin.

Hodder & Stoughton Ltd
Carmelite House
50 Victoria Embankment
London EC4Y 0DZ

www.hodderfaith.com

'My, God, my God, why have you forsaken me?'

Mark 15.34

In the midst of the unbearable story of the passion of the world, we can discover the reconciling story of the passion of Christ.

Jürgen Moltmann[1]

Eloi, Eloi

In strange, exotic words I do not know
you speak of painful things I know too well;
of separation, ever left bereft,
of love forsaken and the grasp of hell.

And it's only fleeting consolation
to find these words embedded in the psalms,
giving meaning to contorted passion,
through the twister's eye a final calm.

God was on the wood that awful Friday
crying out, misunderstood again;
drowning in the depths of our exhaustion,
trouncing pain within the depths of pain.

Twisted thorn and sacred wood and iron,
where life lost, there life has been regained.

CONTENTS

Introduction   1

One   11
Two   23
Three   37
Four   51
Five   63
Six   75
Seven   93

Afterword   109
Acknowledgements   121
Notes   125

INTRODUCTION

We know it was a Friday afternoon. The day before the Sabbath. The scene was just outside the gates of Jerusalem and some people reckon the date might have been 7 April in the year AD 30.

What follows is not of itself anything out of the ordinary: three men are executed by crucifixion; two are criminals, one is a rabbi from Galilee.

So many crucifixions took place at that time that beyond the sordid fascination in watching someone die – sadly crowds have always gathered at gallows – not much was ever remembered of those whose lives were disposed of in this way. But the death of the rabbi from Galilee, Jesus, is still remembered over two thousand years later. It is, for those who follow him, the centre of their faith.

Consequently, more words have been written about this death than any other. This death, so Christians believe, is no mere execution, but the unfolding of God's purposes – humanity reconciled to God. Some of the very first words to be written about it claim that 'though [Jesus] was in the form of God, [he] did not regard equality with God as something to be exploited, but emptied himself, taking the form of a slave . . . And being found in human form, he humbled himself and became obedient to the point of death – even death on a cross' (Philippians 2.6–8).[1]

So this book is just the latest in a long line of sermons, hymns, poems, prayers and writings that help us understand what the death of Jesus means. In particular, this book explores the horrors and anguish of Jesus' dying, to see how it will help us face ours, and all the other forsakenness we see in our world today.

Jesus' death didn't take long. Crucifixion could go on for days. But already severely beaten, Jesus dies after a matter of hours.

In Mark's Gospel we are told that at noon there was darkness over the land for three hours, and at three o'clock the dying man 'cried out with a loud voice, "Eloi, Eloi, lema sabachthani?" which means, "My God, my God, why have you forsaken me?"' (Mark 15.34).

These are his last words.

Some bystanders hear him and say, 'Listen, he is calling for Elijah' (Mark 15.35). One of them fetches a sponge filled with sour wine, puts it on a stick, and gives it to him to drink, saying, 'Wait, let us see whether Elijah will come to take him down' (Mark 15.36). Then Jesus gives another loud cry and breathes his last (Mark 15.37).

In this book, we will explore the meaning of Jesus' death by looking in painful detail at these last words recorded in Mark's Gospel, repeated in Matthew's, but omitted from Luke and not found in John.

A person's last words always hold a certain fascination. Not just those of our loved ones, but also of so-called 'famous people', be it a philosopher, a poet or a soap star. There are whole books and websites dedicated to the topic. We seem to reckon that someone's last words may have some special meaning. We think they might be more than just the full stop at the end of life. Moreover, the greater the person, the more significant the words must be. Or so we imagine. Perhaps they will tell us what that life meant, summing up a lifetime's wisdom and experience.

Actually, very few have such power. The Greek philosopher Epicurus said, 'Farewell, and remember all my words.' But most of what he wrote is lost. Edward I said to his son, 'Carry my bones before you on your march, for the rebels will not be able to endure the sight of me, alive or dead.' But they did manage to endure. Michelangelo said, 'I'm still learning.' The comedian Spike Milligan had the words, 'I told you I was ill', inscribed on his headstone.

But Jesus' last words endure. Books are written about them (like this one). They are the subject of many sermons. However, when we turn to the words themselves, we are presented with a bit of a conundrum.

First of all, we have to decide which ones to choose. Jesus says different things in each of the Gospels.

Second, none of them is easy.

And, third, some of the things he says, like the words this book is examining, are extremely challenging, things we would really rather not hear at all.

This book is about the words we find in Mark's Gospel. Most biblical commentators agree that Mark's account is the earliest. Mark's whole Gospel is dramatic and immediate. There is no birth narrative. Jesus arrives on the stage of human history, a grown man with a divine purpose. The story leads quickly to Jerusalem and a confrontation with the political and religious powers of his day. He appears to be defeated. His death is brutal and quick. His last words are shocking and painful: 'My God, why have you deserted me?'

Even the resurrection in Mark's Gospel is shot through with ambiguity. The tomb is definitely empty. The stone is rolled away. We are told that Jesus is risen. We are told he is no longer in the tomb. However, we don't know where he is, nor quite what has happened, nor what it will mean. The women flee from the tomb seized by terror and amazement.

We will, by the end of this book, come back to the

resurrection, because Jesus' death and his being raised by the Father are two sides of one astonishing reality. But we cannot dodge the cross, nor the hideous cruelty we find there, nor the anguish and horror of Christ's death.

In other words, before we can get to the resurrection, we must stand at the cross. That is what this book will help us do. Moreover, as we stand under the cross, we begin to understand it.

We will hear Jesus crying out. We will stay with these awful words. We will examine them. We will acknowledge their difficulty.

By 'difficulty', I don't mean we can't understand them. They are uttered in another language. But, unlike the bystanders and soldiers who stood there, we have Mark's translation. The meaning is actually very plain, and as Mark Twain famously commented, 'It isn't the bits of the Bible I can't understand that give me the most challenge, it's the bits I can!'

Jesus' words are all too easy to comprehend, and all too difficult to apprehend; that is, we may know what they mean with our heads, but not yet with our hearts. As he dies – and this is the dreadful truth of it – Jesus feels abandoned by the God who had been so close to him in every other aspect of his earthly life. He is not just forsaken. He is 'Godforsaken'.

Again and again in the Hebrew scriptures that Jesus would have known so well (what we call the Old Testament), we hear promises that God will not forsake us if we are faithful to him. So Psalm 37 says that the Lord will 'not forsake his faithful ones' and that 'the righteous shall be kept safe for ever' (Psalm 37.28).

But who could have been more faithful than Jesus? And now it is Jesus who is forsaken.

So, hearing these words on Jesus' lips can't help but cast doubt on the rest of the story. If Jesus finds God absent at the point of death, what hope is there for the rest of us?

And might at least one of the other Gospel authors have had this concern as well?

Even though most biblical commentators conclude that in all

probability Matthew and Luke had a copy of Mark's Gospel – or something very like it – in front of them when they wrote theirs, Matthew keeps these difficult words in, but Luke does not. He omits them.

We don't know why. Perhaps Luke didn't want to confuse the faithful. Perhaps he is drawing on another tradition. Whatever the reason, in his account, Jesus seems more at peace with what is happening. He still cries out in a loud voice, but his final words make his death an offering to God. 'Into your hands I commend my spirit' is his last utterance (Luke 23.46). You won't be surprised to hear that this is also the Gospel in which we find Jesus reaching out to the criminals crucified with him. 'Today you will be with me in Paradise', he says to one of them (Luke 23.43).

John doesn't have the difficult words of Mark either. He may not have read Mark's Gospel – we just don't know – but like Luke, his Gospel portrays Jesus as being much more in control of the situation. As he dies, Jesus declares, 'It is finished' (John 19.30). He then bows his head and gives up his spirit. It is *given up*, not taken away. There is no anguish, just an aching thirst, which seems to be as much for *us* as the consequence of anything that is done to him (though it must be both). This reflects John's vision of the cross as the great triumph of love.[2] On the cross, something has been accomplished. Jesus, it seems, is even reigning from the cross.

Mark and Matthew also believe that something is accomplished here. However, their accounts are different. In particular, they include the distressing and tormented words that are the subject of this book.

So which were the words Jesus actually said? Many will see that as a reasonable question to ask.

We just can't know for sure. Nor do I think we will get very far trying to decide which of the Gospels is the most historically accurate (though we do know that Mark's account is the earliest).

The four Gospels offer four different *and complementary* portraits of Jesus. We need all of them. They enable us to see Jesus from different angles.

Moreover, it is also possible that, drawing on other traditions of preaching and other psalms and Old Testament passages that pre-figured the death of Jesus, Luke and John could be enlarging the story for their own particular reasons and to emphasise the important truth that Jesus' death on the cross *is* a victory. They are, then, no less true, but might not record the words Jesus actually said, in the way that these terrible words from Mark's Gospel must do.

For these words of desolation and desperation could hardly have been made up. After all, if you are telling a story whose opening line is the bold declaration that this is 'The beginning of the good news of Jesus Christ, the Son of God' (Mark 1.1), the one who died and rose again, and if you were thinking of putting some last words into his mouth, you wouldn't have chosen these ones! Jesus, therefore, must have said them. There really is no other credible conclusion.

Of course, Jesus could have said *all* the things we find in the four Gospels. We just can't know this for sure. What we do know is that from quite early times the Church constructed a narrative, which became known as 'The Seven Last Words from the Cross', which piece together all the things that Jesus said from the cross and give them an order. They are often the subject of Good Friday addresses. They have been set to music. The setting by James MacMillan is a particular favourite of mine. I listen to it each Lent and Holy Week.

In this traditional scheme, Jesus' cry of abandonment is placed fourth. Putting it here lessens the painful impact. His more comfortable words from John and Luke come afterwards. It is as if the cry of abandonment was just *a stage on the journey* towards the accomplishment and abandonment to God that John and Luke portray.

But in Mark, it is just these terrifying words. Jesus dies, crying out with heartbreaking anguish. His words are words of bleak desolation. And as we hear them, we wonder whether the meaning of the story we are telling can be true, for Jesus experiences the same terrible abandonment that is our own darkest fear; the darkness we spend so much time avoiding, the darkness we don't want ever to confront: 'My God, my God, why have you forsaken me?'

This book aims simply and steadfastly to plumb the depths of these words, discovering in them a strange and beautiful hope: the hope that Jesus, in his passion and death, has indeed shared the horrors of our own isolation, desperation and alienation from God and from one another. Moreover, his resurrection only brings hope and meaning to our lives precisely because he has participated in such passion and separation.

Along the way, we will discover that this is one of only a handful of occasions in the Gospels where the actual Aramaic that Jesus spoke is preserved. Again, why would this be the case were it not for the fact that this terrible cry of anguish was uttered by Jesus and remembered by those who were there – seared into their memory? So much so that, when the account was written down, they felt compelled to retain those actual words and not just their translation.

Second, we will discover that these words are a quotation. They are the opening line of Psalm 22. In some respects, this also softens their blow; Jesus is reciting the scriptures, and Psalm 22, in particular, offers what the early Church came to understand as a commentary on the passion of Christ.

Third, we will discover how the words have always been misunderstood, or, perhaps, not looked at as forensically as we shall do here.

Finally, we will explore what they tell us about God, and how we find our identity and purpose as those who are united with Christ in his death and resurrection.

Although some of this book began life as a series of Good Friday meditations preached in St Wilfrid's, Chichester over thirty years ago, the vast majority of it has been written in 2019, 2020, 2021 and 2022; that is, during the coronavirus pandemic, some of it appearing in Holy Week meditations in Chelmsford Cathedral and York Minster.

It isn't particularly a Covid book, but I'm not sure it would have been written quite like this if it weren't for the isolation all of us have experienced in the last couple of years, nor the unwelcome, but probably necessary, confrontation with our frailty and mortality that Covid has brought us.

Each chapter looks at the words themselves from different perspectives, but then includes stories and meditations that take the themes of the chapter and explores them from the standpoint of those who come to the cross, or those who look at it with curious longing from afar. In this way you will hear my own voice as I look at the cross, and contemplate death, and wonder what death and resurrection mean, but I also bring with me other people I have met, ministered to and received from, or others I have read about. You will hear about my passion as well as the passion of Christ. Through all this, as we read the book, we will gather round the cross.

I invite you, then, to stand with me, and with those I will bring with me, and with those you will be carrying in your hearts. Together, we will look and learn.

Our whole world needs to be built differently. It cries out in its own agony for a different set of values, an identity that is something more than the ones we create for ourselves or are imposed on us by others, and for a sense of belonging. The painful singularity of Christ on the cross offers a place to start: this rejected stone can become again the foundation of who we are and the world we wish to build.

'Naked I came from my mother's womb, and naked shall I return there; the Lord gave, and the Lord has taken away; blessed be the name of the Lord' (Job 1.21) are Job's famous words in the eponymous Old Testament book that is itself such a painfully pronounced reflection on suffering. This is where Jesus was led, and this is where we will endeavour to travel as well.

Few people have made Jesus' cry of dereliction their own last words, though many will have felt that way, and many of us fear that, in the end, this is what death will hold for us: just isolation, despair and a dread finality.

Many others, including Lady Jane Grey and Mary Queen of Scots before being beheaded, Thomas Cranmer before being burned at the stake, Christopher Columbus and Charlemagne, opted for Jesus' words from Luke's Gospel when they died: 'Father, into your hands I commend my spirit' (Luke 23.46). They were in good company. The first Christian martyr, Stephen, did the same thing in an account also written by Luke, though now he asks Jesus, not the Father, to receive his spirit (see Acts 7.59).

What this book aims for is more like the final words of Joan of Arc. As the fires were lit around her, she asked that the cross be held high so that she could see it through the flames.

~

At the end of each chapter are some questions.

These can be used to help you reflect on what you've just read and lead you deeper into the story. You don't have to do this, but if you are reading the book with others as part of a Lent group, Book group or Home group – or just with one or two friends – give yourselves about an hour to share your reflections.

Here is a simple pattern you could follow:

- Read Mark 15.33–9.
- Share reflections or observations on the passage or anything else about the passage or the book that has occurred to you during the week.

- Go through the questions at the end of the chapter.
- Read one of the poems on p. ix or 117.
- Finish with prayer.

This prayer in particular may help gather together all we are exploring:

> Blessed are you, Lord God of our salvation,
> to you be praise and glory for ever.
> As a man of sorrows and acquainted with grief
> your only Son was lifted up
> that he might draw the whole world to himself.
> May we walk this day in the way of the cross
> and always be ready to share its weight,
> declaring your love for all the world.
> Blessed be God, Father, Son and Holy Spirit.
> Blessed be God forever.[3]

ONE

**It is wise to remember that
Jesus didn't speak English.**

When the scriptures are read in church and the reader declares, 'This is the Word of the Lord', it is the word of the Lord that has gone through several translations.

First of all, there are the many English translations, from the Venerable Bede who translated John's Gospel into Old English in the eighth century, through John Wycliffe in the fourteenth (who made a second-hand translation via the Latin Vulgate) and William Tyndale in the sixteenth, who was able to go back to the original Greek. Each one rests upon, and to some extent relies upon, what has gone before. Some of Tyndale's phrases in particular – 'lick the dust', 'go the extra mile', 'signs of the times' and 'pour out your heart' – to name a few – not only passed into the Authorised Version of 1611 but from that into public consciousness and are still used today. Moreover, once someone has become only moderately familiar with the Bible, it is impossible for certain phrases not to remain fixed in the mind. These words and phrases *are the Word of God for us*, and if we find them translated differently there is an uncomfortable jolt.

Perhaps the best example of this is the beatitudes, the famous text from the beginning of the Sermon on the Mount in Matthew's Gospel.[1] The New English Bible of the 1970s translated the Greek word that we usually translate as 'blessed' as 'happy'. This caused consternation. For hundreds of years the English ear had been used to one word. Now it was replaced by another, which to many minds said something different altogether. The 'behappytudes' moaned one elderly member of the congregation where I was serving at the time. However, both translations are accurate.

Because it is, of course, a translation. The New Testament was written in Greek, not English. This is the unchanging text. It is the constant upon which all the variants in English (and other languages) are built. Therefore, students of biblical theology, and most clergy, study the New Testament in Greek. And even if they have only a slender grasp of the language, in this case a little bit of knowledge does go a long way, for you don't have to learn much of any language before quickly discovering all the challenges, opportunities and pitfalls that are involved in translation. So the Greek word *makarios* carries both the English meaning of 'being blessed' *and* the meaning of 'being happy'. In fact, the Greek word is kind of saying that true happiness can only come from true blessedness and by doing what God wants and living how God expects. But we don't have one English word that does both these things, so the translator has to make a choice, and because that choice in this instance had traditionally been 'blessed', when people heard the word 'happy' being used instead they felt someone had been tampering with the text. But they hadn't. They were just bringing out another aspect of meaning.

Take another example: the very simple, but hugely significant, English word 'love'. For us, it carries multiple meanings, and we work out the meaning from the context of the sentence. So when I say, for instance, 'I love my wife', or when I say, 'I love pizza', you are instantly able to interpret what I say and – as it were – fill in the gaps, i.e. that there is more than one type of love. The love for a spouse is different from the love for pizza. You know this and understand this, but you have to do the work of interpretation yourself, because in English we only have the one word.

In Greek, there are multiple[2] words for love, and therefore none of them can be precisely translated by the single English word love. The translator is going to have to provide some context. Either that, or miss the meaning of the Greek text.

Philia is a rather general word for love, for better or worse. The Bible uses it for the love that God the Father has for Christ (John 5.20), but it's also used when Jesus criticises religious leaders for loving the best seats in the synagogue (Matthew 23.6), and for the love of money that is 'a root of all kinds of evil' (1 Timothy 6.10). *Agapé*, on the other hand, almost always means unconditional love that is blessed with goodness: God's love for humanity (John 3.16), and the caring love that people have that's directed towards the good of others.

Sometimes it works the other way round, as with *makarios*: Greek has one word where we have two or three. Let me offer another example. Because the Hebrew thought world that Jesus inhabited used the same words flexibly to apply to physical and spiritual ideas, the Bible's word *sozo*, which is usually translated in English as 'save', could just as accurately be translated 'rescue' or 'heal'. In Greek and Hebrew thought the two concepts are united. In English thought and English language, they are separate. A *sozo* word is used when the disciples ask Jesus to *rescue* them from a storm (Matthew 8.25), when Jairus asks Jesus to *heal* his daughter (Mark 5.23), and when Paul writes about people believing in Christ, '*saved*' in a religious sense (1 Corinthians 1.21).

This also creates some interesting challenges for translation and interpretation. Famous texts like Jesus' words to Zacchaeus could just as well be translated 'health has come to this house' as 'salvation has come' (see Luke 19.9). For the Greek and Hebrew minds, there is no problem. For us, there is.

We don't know whether Jesus himself spoke Greek – he might have done, because it was a 'get by' language in much of the Roman empire – but day by day he would have spoken a different language. In the Bible, his words have been translated from another language into Greek. That language was Aramaic, which belongs to the same family as Hebrew, and Jesus spoke it in a form that doesn't really exist today, though if you remember Mel Gibson's salaciously gory film of the life of Christ, he did have Jesus speaking Aramaic throughout – with a subtitled English translation.

However, there are one or two places in the New Testament where the Aramaic that Jesus actually spoke – the actual words, with the very particular meanings that they had within that language, and the sounds and music that those words made in the mouth and on the ear – remain. It is as if, in these few instances, the particular words so imprinted themselves on the minds of those who first heard them that even if they didn't speak Aramaic themselves (though, more likely, they knew Aramaic well), when they came to tell their story to others or to have it written down by others, they just couldn't let go of the actual words; the sounds that were rolling round their heads and fixed in their memory. They couldn't bring themselves to just translate them, as they had done with most of the things Jesus said. These particular words had somehow been so powerful and so memorable that they had stuck. It was, therefore, much better that the reader learned a little bit of Aramaic, rather than lose the words in their translation to another language.

So when Jesus raises Jairus' daughter to life he says to her, in Aramaic, '*Talitha cum*', and Mark provides the translation, 'Little girl, get up!' (Mark 5.41). And when the deaf man's ears are opened, Jesus looks up to heaven, and sighs and says to him, '"Ephphatha", that is, "Be opened"' (Mark 7.34). There are others, such as the word '*Hosanna*' that we shout out on Palm Sunday and every Sunday in the Eucharistic liturgy, meaning 'Please save us' (see Mark 11). Or the great prayer and hope of the early Church, and our hope too: '*Maranatha*', which means, 'Lord, come!' (see 1 Corinthians 16.22). And there are a couple of moments of great personal intensity when the Gospel writers kept other people's Aramaic: Bartimaeus, asking Jesus to restore his sight (Mark 10.51), and Mary Magdalene on Easter morning (John 20.16) both address Jesus as '*Rabbouni*', 'My teacher!'

But the most famous and most significant are the words Jesus spoke from the cross.

This is how Mark puts it in what is the earliest account of the passion that we have: 'When it was noon, darkness came over the whole land until three in the afternoon. At three o'clock Jesus cried out with a loud voice, "Eloi, Eloi, lema sabachthani?"' (Mark 15.33–4).

Then comes the translation: terrible, beautiful words; words whose depths we will seek to plumb in this book, though we will never get to the bottom of them: 'My God, my God, why have you forsaken me?'

What do these words mean?

Does Jesus on the cross suffer the same terrible isolation from God that is my darkest fear?

Does he die abandoned, and if so what does the cross really mean? Is it, after all, just one more lonely death?

We translate *sabachthani* as forsaken. Sometimes the word 'abandoned' or 'deserted' is chosen. But because of its connotation of not just being alone, but of being separated from the one you need the most and to be completely given up, even left behind, forsaken is probably the best English translation. This, unflinchingly, is what St Mark says that Jesus experienced. The words are in his mouth. And because they are these strange Aramaic words, we can do little other than conclude that they are the words Jesus said and therefore the words we must wrestle with.

~

When my children were teenagers, our house, being larger than most, was invariably the gathering place for them and their friends. I'm not sure this is what the Church Commissioners of the Church of England had in mind when they put bishops in fairly large houses, but it was not an uncommon experience for me to get up in the morning and have to tread over and tiptoe round the sleeping bodies of various adolescents who had come home late with one of my sons and crashed out on the settee or on the floor.

Actually, I loved it. It wasn't without its frustrations and challenges, but it is energising and exciting to have young people about the place, particularly as the vast majority of my sons' friends had had little or nothing to do with the Church and were more fascinated by what I did than my sons cared to admit. Late-night conversations were often about matters of faith, purpose and identity. As well as football, that is.

When my middle son was about twelve or thirteen, just entering into the cusp and challenge of adolescence, there was a regular visitor to our house; let's call him James. He was a polite, slightly awkward, slightly serious boy, finding his way into life and straining at the leash of his upbringing. We were round the kitchen table one afternoon after school having a cup of tea and he was reflecting on the different faith identities of people he knew. I was Bishop of Reading at the time. Our children went to the local comprehensive, which served the very diverse communities of West Reading. This is one bit of the Royal County of Berkshire that is under the radar of its comfortable affluence.

James said to me, 'So you're Christians', and then he said that another of his friends at school was a Muslim, and another a Jew. 'But what am I?' he said.

There was a plaintive sadness in his words.

He had observed that some of his friends, even those like my middle son who at the time was hardly a model of Christian discipleship and who was also, as is quite natural, chafing at the bit of his upbringing, had an identity that was rooted in a tradition and that gave him a place of belonging and a name.

He had seen that some people were Christians and therefore followers of Jesus Christ and therefore members of a community, which was both local and universal. Or you were a Muslim and part of that tradition. Or a Jew. Or a Hindu.

But he didn't have that kind of identity, community or tradition. And he'd noticed it. His parents, good people though they were, had themselves not been brought up in any faith tradition themselves. They had a set of values, no doubt, but it was only very fleetingly rooted in a set of beliefs; and even if it was, belief in those beliefs had only been a lived reality at least a couple of generations ago. James was probably two generations unchurched.

As it happens, I was brought up in a similar household. My parents would have certainly called themselves Christian, and I, like my sister and brothers, was baptised as an infant (I went to church at least once!). But we didn't go again. The Christian values by which we lived were rooted in the Christian faith, though not in any obvious or conscious way. Nor were they nurtured in the living tradition of a community through worship and fellowship, which is the best – perhaps the only – bulwark against the steady erosion of these values.

Sitting round our kitchen table that afternoon, I don't think James was *knowingly* articulating a train of thought that had led him to this conclusion, but he intuitively saw in some of his friends something he didn't have himself and it was a cause of sorrow. 'What am I?' he said.

And I suppose the answer is that he is a child of a largely tolerant, liberal, democratic, secular materialist worldview whose values are actually quite close to the Christian faith (how could it be otherwise, for it is the Christian faith that has done more than anything else to shape British and European culture), but which lacks the defining rituals and traditions, still less the lived experience of the knowledge of God, which constitutes belonging and shapes and preserves the values. Because I am part of this tradition, I can say I am a Christian (even with all the doubts and anxieties all people of faith always carry with them). So could my parents, and possibly his, because they may have had some lingering sense of Christian faith inside them.

But James couldn't. He didn't feel he belonged to anything that could form his identity beyond himself. He knew he was an individual, and I suppose he knew he was a member of a family, a local community and a nation. But it wasn't enough. And he knew it. And because so much emphasis is put on 'being an individual' and 'finding fulfilment' and even – heaven help us! – 'finding your own truth' that, like the burning coal that once taken out of the fire quickly goes out, it was beginning to dawn on him that being an individual wasn't quite enough. He also seemed to have an inbuilt sense that truth did exist. And also right and wrong.

He felt forsaken. Forsaken by the culture that had nurtured him and, perhaps, even 'godforsaken' by the Christian tradition (and perhaps other faith traditions?) that had failed to draw him in. I don't know. All I do know is that in the cry of his heart that day I heard the cry of our whole culture where so many of us, regardless of our wealth or position, feel an aching loneliness and even an emptiness; that living by a certain set of values, even if we do it well, is not enough. We crave some greater belonging. We feel the aching loss of something we intuitively know is ours, but can't quite get hold of. Our hearts are restless, as St Augustine famously put it, until they find their rest in God.

There is also here a question of interpretation and failure of interpretation.

How do we translate into the cultures and languages of today, the story, beliefs and values that we see and receive in Jesus Christ? What remains constant? What changes? And how have we failed to do this, so that young people like James can grow up longing for something that they can register as real, but can't grasp hold of. It has left them behind. Or, perhaps, for whatever reason, it might be more accurate to say, the culture has left it behind, the Church doesn't know quite how to share it, and people like James are left stranded in its wake, forever catching the scent of something they know, but can't quite place, still less return to.

Questions

1. What is your immediate response to Jesus' words from the cross?
2. What does the word 'forsaken' mean to you, and have you experienced being forsaken?
3. What would you like to say to James to help him find identity in Christ? Why not put down on paper what you'd say were you to write him a letter?
4. What more could the Church be doing to come alongside people like James?

TWO

'My God, my God, why have you forsaken me?'
is the opening line of Psalm 22.

TWO

Jesus dies, it turns out, with the words of scripture on his lips. He spoke them in Aramaic, his mother tongue, but, to add another language into the mix: he would have also known them in their original Hebrew.[1] It's interesting, but not surprising, that Jesus uses the Aramaic text, because translations from classical biblical Hebrew were in use in his time. I have a feeling that all of us who may know more than one language will turn to our mother tongue at hours of need. These are words Jesus may well have learned as a child: in the home and in the synagogue. They resourced him in this hour of most desperate need and agony.

This doesn't mean the words don't still chill us with their horror. Jesus is still crying out that God has abandoned him. But, as many commentators on this passage point out, as they are the opening verse of Psalm 22 they should be understood and interpreted in the context of the psalm itself as well as in the psalm's new context, spoken from the cross.

The words are still painful; Jesus remains in great agony; but now we can add another dimension to his cry of dereliction: Jesus is drawing on the Psalms, and with them his whole religious tradition, upbringing and formation. The words that give voice to his forsakeneness are the words of the scriptures he knows and loves. They also comfort him through the agony, perhaps even helping him make sense of what is happening. He has an identity within a religious tradition. He draws on it.

This is certainly what the early Church did. In fact, when we read Psalm 22 it seems to be a commentary on the passion. And if you haven't read Psalm 22 recently, have a look at it. You will probably be surprised. It seems to be predicting what would happen on the cross, even some of its smallest details. Hence, we find phrases like:

> I am poured out like water, and all my bones are out of joint; my heart is like wax; it is melted within my breast; my mouth is dried up like a potsherd, and my tongue sticks to my jaws; you lay me in the dust of death.

(PSALM 22.14–15)

And later on:

> They pierce my hands and my feet.

(PSALM 22.16)

What does this tell us?

Well, first of all, it tells us that Jesus loved the Psalms: that he knew the Psalms; that they were woven into his life of prayer. He probably knew many of them by heart. This in turn tells us about the place of the Psalms within the community of faith, the Jewish community that Jesus belonged to.

The Psalms have always held a central place in Christian devotion and worship. This is also true for the Jewish faith. The Psalms are the prayer book of the Bible. Perhaps, the hymn book, too. So, for instance, you may have noticed that in the Bible itself there are little notes, usually printed in small italics, indicating how the Psalms were sung within the worship of the temple and later the synagogue. Psalm 30, we are told, is 'A Song at the dedication of the temple'. Worship leaders are told that Psalm 4 is 'with stringed instruments', while Psalm 5 is 'for the flutes'. And so on. Therefore, when we sing and say these same psalms in church we are participating in a vast tradition of prayer and praise that joins our voices to countless millions of Christian and Jewish voices going back through the centuries.

And it is impossible to outdo the Psalms. There is something for every situation and predicament. Only more so. If you are feeling angry, you will find a psalm that is angrier than you. If you are feeling desolate, you will find a psalm that is more desolate than you. If you are feeling joyful and filled with praise, you will find a psalm that is more joyful than you. If you are feeling alienated or alone, there is a psalm that is more isolated than you.

Psalm 55[2] speaks of the bitterness of betrayal:

> For it was not an open enemy that reviled me,
> For then I could have borne it;
> Nor was it my adversary that puffed himself up against me,
> For then I would have hid myself from him.
> But it was even you, one like myself,
> My companion and my own familiar friend.

(PSALM 55.12—13)

Nor does it shrink from the strong desire to flee away from distress:

> . . . O that I had wings like a dove,
> For then I would fly away and be at rest . . .
> I would make haste to escape . . .

(PSALM 55.6—7)

Or the hunger for revenge:

> Let death come suddenly upon them;
> Let them go down alive to the Pit.

(PSALM 55.15)

And this is relatively mild, compared with some of the Psalms. The otherwise perfectly lovely Psalm 139, which is all about knowing and being known, suddenly breaks off, spitting with rage against God's enemies and saying how the psalmist has 'nothing but hatred for them' (v.22).

Psalm 88 barely seems to believe in God at all, except for the reality of being rejected by God and the horrors that go with it. It is a psalm of unremitting despair.

None of this is the false comfort that tells us 'not to worry because someone somewhere is worse off than you'. Rather, it is an astonishing scaling of heights and plumbing of depths whereby the Psalms themselves express and expand every possible sentiment and desire about life lived in community with God. As such they endure. And because they include hatred and revenge, they're not easy. But they are real. They fire the imagination; they fuel our praise; they provide text and narrative when we have nothing else to say.

Like a lovesick teenager restless with desire, Psalm 63 cries out, 'O God, you are my God; eagerly I seek you; my soul is athirst for you. My flesh faints for you, as in a dry and thirsty land where there is no water' (vv.1–2).

From the heartbreak of exile, the defeated and dispossessed cry out, 'How shall we sing the Lord's song in a strange land?' (Psalm 137.4).

They are, therefore, incredibly human, encompassing and expressing every human emotion. They do not shy away from darkness. They do not limit praise. They do not flinch from giving voice in the presence of God to the full range of human feeling, including revenge. And they do it in the presence of God, directed to God, speaking to God, honouring God, but speaking to God *as we would speak to each other*. This is the reason that they are a way of praying and a library of prayer. When desolation, forsakenness, elation or torpor leave me not knowing what to say, the Psalms are there for me. They give words that speak to my situation, honed and hallowed by the countless other human voices that have also turned to them for solace.

They were there for Jesus as he hung dying on the cross.
He turned to them.

They helped him pray. They gave him words.

They helped him make sense of what was happening. Of course, for Jesus, as we shall go on to explore, this was not just the physical pain of crucifixion, but also the mental and spiritual anguish of feeling isolated from God.

Psalm 22 speaks into this experience.

Jesus found in this psalm words that both gave voice to his feelings *and* helped him through the hours of his passion. They can help us too.

~

In Shakespeare's play *Hamlet*, Ophelia is criticised by Hamlet's mother for failing to find words of her own as she died. In her final moments she is found chanting 'snatches of old tunes as one incapable of her own distress'.[3] But she did, at least, have some words inside her.

A few centuries later, the distressed youth at the heart of Peter Shaffer's play *Equus* chants advertising jingles to his psychiatrist. They are the only words he has inside him that he knows by heart. He is a child of that first generation where learning things by rote was frowned upon, and where the echo chamber of his mind was stuffed with everything else he heard repetitiously (and is therefore able to draw upon in times of stress), even though the words themselves meant nothing other than 'buy me' and 'desire me'.

I, too, am a child of this generation – and not the product of the sort of expensive education that would have side-stepped this experiment. Neither was I brought up going to church, where, at least until recently, a set liturgy, be it Cranmer or Stancliffe, was unavoidably pressed into your consciousness by the heartbeat of its weekly reiteration.

I think I only learned one poem by heart as a boy – Hilaire Belloc's 'Matilda'. It is quite long, but I could recite it for you now if you asked me. It has become part of me.

Young minds soak things up. Especially words. Especially words with rhythm, metre, verve and rhyme. They are stored in a place where there is always ready access for retrieval; though storing new material gets harder as the years pass by. So, I still know 'Matilda', and could have known so much more, but it's getting harder to lay down new stocks, even if I try.

Like the desperate youth in *Equus*, babbling out the advertising jingles, I was given nothing of lasting value to lay down for the service of a lifetime, that would lift my understanding of life, and help shape my thoughts and dreams.

Oh, how different it used to be.

I remember some of the housebound home communicants I have served in my ministry as a priest. Bessie, living with the terrible mental myopia of dementia, who would chatter incessantly, calling every priest who visited her 'Fr Nicholas', since this was the last one she actually remembered, would suddenly, miraculously, click into her old, 'real self' as soon as the liturgy began, the clamour of her babble becoming, in an instant, the prose and cadences of the Prayer Book that she had known by heart since a girl; or Maud, about whom you will hear more later, who would kneel on the doorstep as I arrived with the sacrament, and knew all the Collects of the Prayer Book by heart; or Blanche, who also knew the Collects and most of the liturgy, but could also recite great passages from scripture by heart, and had within her, also learned in childhood, a little library of poems to draw on as a means of making sense of and giving voice to the dramas and vicissitudes of life. When she knew she was dying, I sat by her bed in the hospital and she recited to me Tennyson's famous poem, 'Crossing the Bar', the one that he wrote three years before his death, instructing that it always be printed as the final poem in any published collection of his verse. Hopeful that there will be no anguish at the point of death, it ends with the lines:

> I hope to see my Pilot face to face
> When I have crost the bar.[4]

And then, more recently, I was travelling by train with Christine, the very able and experienced Chair of the Diocesan Safeguarding Group in Chelmsford diocese, and telling her my half-written ideas for a sermon I was preaching later that day about the gospel as beautiful music that could drown out and overcome the siren voices and snares of the world, in the same way that Orpheus – as we read in Homer's *Odyssey* – played his lyre and drowned out the siren's bewitching songs and enabled Jason to make safe passage; and quick as a flash she was reciting to me from memory, and as it turned out virtually word for word, the song Queen Katherine sings in William Shakespeare's *Henry VIII* when her heart was weary. The song ends with these words of comfort for those facing tribulation:

> In sweet music is such art,
> Killing care and grief of heart
> Fall asleep, or hearing, die.[5]

This is all quite remarkable. And largely lost. Though never so lost that other things do not sink in and occupy the vacant space, and then, when needed, rise up.

We see this in football matches. It is almost a religious experience to go to Anfield and hear the crowd sing 'You'll never walk alone' before the match commences. Even a Spurs fan like me was powerfully moved when I attended. This song has so shaped the culture, history and ethos of that football club through years of success, and through the harrowing tragedy of Hillsborough, that fans have it sung at baptisms, weddings and funerals. It has become a kind of credal anthem for scouse identity. It means so much more than its words. It says 'I belong'; 'I am here'; 'I am part of this'. Though, if the words are about walking together, this of course helps.

'I'm for ever blowing bubbles', while confirming the same identity to West Ham fans, and also sung at baptisms and weddings, does not, even the most ardent Hammer would have to concede, carry the same emotional charge. The words do matter, even when the shared experience of the song takes you beyond them.

At the Rugby, even we English turn a song penned for the oppressed into a psalm of our own. This can't just be because we're good at losing: 'I looked over Jordan, what did I see? Coming for to carry me home. A band of angels, coming after me. Coming for to carry me home. Swing low, sweet chariot, coming for to carry me home.'[6] It expresses a longing and *a belonging*, which unite and comfort in equal measure.

And it isn't just sporting crowds proclaiming identity that sing these songs and make them their own. When he was composing his great anti-war oratorio, that beautiful, anguished cry for peace, *A Child of Our Time,* no less a figure than Sir Michael Tippett turned to African American spirituals, hymnic protest songs, and used them to punctuate the drama of the piece in the same way that Bach's chorales draw the whole audience (or is it a congregation?) into his great passions. So, at the end of the piece, when the choir stands with the soloists to sing, 'Deep River, my home is over Jordan', it is a spine-tinglingly wonderful moment. He, an atheist, makes these slave songs, themselves steeped in scripture, a universal cry for peace and justice.

Why, then, is Hamlet's mother so scornful of Ophelia's inability to find her own words for her own grief? For, surely, something is happening here that is about the deep formation of memory and identity? It is wonderfully comforting, and so much better than an advertising jingle, and charged with the same emotional power as a Bach chorale or an African American spiritual or packed crowd at Anfield: Ophelia had words inside her that she had learned from old songs. They sustain her at the hour of death and enable her to give voice to her distress.

We don't know what those old songs were. However, they might have been the Psalms, because this is how the Psalms work. They are the old songs we used to know well. They are the songs we could know again.

So central were they to the theology and worship of some Eastern Orthodox denominations that it used to be required of those holding ecclesiastical office in the Church that they know the Psalter by heart. Those being formed in theological colleges and courses in the Church of England today are not subject to such a strict regime. A few charismatic choruses will suffice. But what a gift to mind and spirit, to receive and know the Psalter by heart, and to be able to draw upon its riches of poetry and thought so that one's own words and prayers are shaped by this praying, and are there for you when your own words fail.

It is good to say the words that others have said. They give the words additional meaning. However, it would be a mistake to think that the Psalms are only valuable because of their age, or because so many people have said them over so many centuries. They carry passionate conviction, exuberance and joy not just because they are old. Thomas Merton has said that in the Psalms 'we drink divine praise at its pure stainless source, in all its primitive sincerity and perfection'.[7] In other words, the Psalms are *young*. They give voice to the people of God's youthful strength and directness. This is why they endure.

Just as Ophelia found comfort in the words that others had written and sung, so this was true for Jesus as he died. His cry of anguish in Mark's Gospel, 'My God, my God, why have you forsaken me?' (Mark 15.34), is, as we have seen, the opening line of Psalm 22. His final words in Luke's Gospel, 'Father, into your hands I commit my spirit' (Luke 23.46) are from Psalm 31.[8] Even his words in John's Gospel, 'I am thirsty' (John 19.28), allude to the Psalms, possibly Psalm 143.6: 'I stretch out my hands to you; my soul thirsts for you like a parched land . . .' or Psalm 22.15: 'My mouth is dried up like a potsherd, and my tongue sticks to my jaws; you lay me in the dust of death' or Psalm 69.3: 'I am weary with my crying; my throat is parched . . .'

Not only do we not learn poems or Shakespeare or virtually anything by heart nowadays – why would you need to bother learning something, when you can just google it! – but the spiritual and liturgical disciplines that were so much a part of the Christian formation of our forebears have fallen into disuse.

One of the axioms of the contemporary church seems to be that somehow prayer can only be heartfelt if it is extempore. The Old Testament is read less and less in church; and whereas in former times the biblical diet of worship always included a psalm, in some churches they are hardly read at all in the main Sunday worship. Indeed, I did go to a charismatic evangelical church recently – which had better remain nameless – where there was no Bible reading at all! On the one hand, this is shocking, but it is also only a logical extension of a certain way of worshipping where the testimony of individual faith and ecstatic experience takes central place. It may be peppered with biblical quotations and biblically based choruses, but there is not only no systematic reading of scripture, which was the bedrock of the Prayer Book liturgy, but also in this case no reading of scripture at all. On their deathbed this congregation will have snatches of choruses, but not the songs of scripture.

'A Christian community without the Psalter has lost an incomparable treasure,' wrote Dietrich Bonhoeffer; 'and by taking it back into use will recover resources it never dreamed it had.'[9]

Martin Luther once complained that many people's prayers seemed to him to be trifling little devotions. 'There is none of the sap, the strength, the fervour and the fire that I find in the Psalms,' he said.

As we look at Jesus on the cross, as we hear him cry out these terrible words of forsakenness, we experience the heat and fire of the Psalms.

This is the reason I love them. This is the reason the Church needs them. They are the old songs that we all need to sing, the songs that are also always energetically young. They give voice to our deepest feelings and aspirations before God. They give us words and phrases that can express the inchoate feelings and aspirations that might otherwise remain unexpressed. At the same time, they give permission for our joy to be exuberant, our frustration to be uninhibited, and our anger to be released.

Learning a psalm by heart – or even a few verses of a psalm – will help express and shape this desire for God, as will learning other prayers and poems. It gets harder as you get older, but it is not impossible.

But if you do this – if you make the effort to learn something like this by heart – you will be giving yourself a gift that can be unwrapped on your deathbed. Something to support you and carry you through life's final hours. As it did for Jesus.

Questions

1. Are there any poems, songs, pieces of scripture or prayers that you know by heart? When did you learn them? When do you turn to them? Can your share them?
2. Do you have a favourite psalm? And why?
3. How does it change your understanding of Jesus' words from the cross when you discover he is quoting Psalm 22?
4. Why not have a go at writing a psalm yourself? Or something like a psalm – a prayer or a short verse that gives voice to your feelings and longings.

THREE

Because Jesus' terrible cry of dereliction is the opening verse of Psalm 22 it leads us into this psalm *in its entirety*, and helps us understand what the cross means.

Psalm 22 begins to outline the theological response to the cross, which becomes the basis of the Church's teaching.

The early Church and the New Testament authors came to believe that by saying these words Jesus is helping us to understand that his death on the cross is in fulfilment of scripture, which for them, of course, meant the prophecies of the Hebrew Bible, what we call the Old Testament.

It is also wise for us to remember that the crucifixion was a stumbling block for the first followers of Jesus. It is hard for us to imagine this. For those of us who call ourselves Christian, the cross is self-evidently the centre of our faith. For the first Christians it was a problem: Messiahs didn't suffer and die!

The first Christians were all good Jews. They therefore believed that the Messiah would come as a conquering hero. Rather like a new King David, he would kick out the Romans and establish a new Jewish kingdom, free from foreign rule and oppression. So when Jesus died on the cross it seemed to them that this only proved they were mistaken: he couldn't be the Messiah.

This explains the much-loved and beautiful story of the encounter on the Emmaus Road, when Cleopas and his companion leave Jerusalem and encounter a stranger who asks them what has been happening in Jerusalem. They tell the stranger about Jesus and how they 'had hoped that he was the one to redeem Israel' (Luke 24.21). It is an astonishing story. Here they are, on the first Easter Day, talking to the Risen Jesus, but they don't recognise him. Their sadness and unbelief, and his mysterious risen presence that is different in appearance from what some might imagine is a resuscitated corpse, not to mention his yearning to allow them to put the pieces together themselves, *prevent* them from recognising him. But they have all the information they need. They know about the cross. They know the prophecies from scripture that speak about a Messiah. They even know about the resurrection. They have him standing at their side. But none of it is good news for them. This is because they cannot conceive of a Messiah who would suffer. And they don't believe in resurrection. It is their *faith*, the very faith they have been taught and faithfully adhere to, that doesn't allow it, not some inner lack of belief or trust.

So what does Jesus do? He listens to them carefully. He chides them for their slowness, but, primarily, he teaches them: he takes them back inside their own tradition and 'beginning with Moses and all the prophets, he interpreted to them the things about himself in all the scriptures' (Luke 24.27). In other words, he shows them that everything that has happened was, after all, not a *denial* of their scripture, but its *fulfilment*. It happened in accordance with scripture, but not as they had ever understood it.

This then becomes a major theme for the early Church in its preaching of the gospel to fellow Jews. They show that what happened to Jesus was according to God's plan, and therefore revealed in scripture. Even the crucifixion. And once they had established this new interpretation of scripture, they were able to go further, and see how certain texts pre-figured the passion and death of Christ. Certain psalms were particularly relevant.

And of course they turned to Psalm 22, precisely because they remembered Jesus' cry of dereliction, and they find there words that enable them to tell and understand the whole story.

So, as we have already noted, v.16 says: 'They pierce my hands and my feet.'

Actually, the precise translation of the Hebrew text is unclear. (As we are discovering, translation is rarely straightforward.) Does it mean 'pierce' or does it mean 'shrivelled'? Of course, because Jesus dies with the first verse of this psalm on his lips, and because *he had indeed been pierced* in his hands and his feet, the Church was clear what the translation should be and therefore saw the psalm as a pre-figuring of the passion.

Hence the other key verse, 'They divide my clothes among themselves, and for my clothing they cast lots' (Psalm 22.18), can be understood in two ways: a remarkable anticipation of one of the details of the passion story; or the Church telling the story through the lens of the psalm that they have already agreed pre-figures the passion.

This is not the same as making it up. Rather it shows how, having established that Jesus' death is in accordance with scripture, scripture, as well as the events themselves, become the means through which the story can be told, and by which its true meaning is revealed. They draw on scripture in order to tell the story and reveal its truth: namely, that all this happened *in accordance with God's will*, and therefore *in accordance with scripture*.

John emphasises the point by even using this formula – 'in accordance with scripture' – in his Gospel. He of course uses the example of the soldiers dividing Jesus' clothes among themselves (see John 19.24–5). But in John's Gospel, Jesus thirsts not just because he is thirsty, but because his thirsting fulfils the scriptures (see John 19.28). And later on when he tells us that not one of his bones is broken and that they will look upon the one they have pierced (see John 19.32–7), he says this happens *so that scriptures should be fulfilled.*

What scriptures? Well, in this case, Psalm 34.20: 'He keeps all their bones; not one of them will be broken.' And, unsurprisingly, Psalm 22: 'I can count all my bones. They stare and gloat over me' (Psalm 22.17). Indeed, this little phrase – in accordance with scripture – becomes so significant that it even finds its way into the creeds and Sunday by Sunday we find ourselves reciting it: 'For us and for our salvation he came down from heaven . . . he suffered death and was buried . . . on the third day he rose again *in accordance with the Scriptures*.'[1]

Finally, to hear these words on the lips of Jesus as he dies tells us something vital about his passion and death, and also helps us consider how we will face our own passion and mortality.

Jesus is the one who thirsts. He thirsts because he is dying and because he is in unimaginable pain. Crucifixion was a terrible and tortuous form of death. The condemned man would shift his weight from nailed wrist to nailed ankle, relieving the pressure and the pain from one part of his dehydrating body to another, and sometimes it would take days to die. That is why in John's Gospel the soldiers are sent to break the legs of those being crucified. It was an act of mercy, hastening death.

And Jesus thirsts because he is the one who has come to do God's will. He thirsts to do what he must do, which is that thing which we could never do for ourselves, and so become the Lamb of God, the perfect offering that we could not make ourselves: 'Am I not to drink the cup that the Father has given me?' says Jesus in John's Gospel (John 18.11). Having struggled in Gethsemane to be reconciled to the Father's will, he is now ready to drain it to the dregs, however painful and however horrifying.

He thirsts for us. He does this in our place. He does this to show us what perfect love and perfect mercy looks like: 'Father, forgive them' (Luke 23.34) are the first words from the cross, words of astonishing kindness and forgiveness. This is what turning the other cheek, walking the second mile, loving your enemies looks like.

At the end there is real horror and real anguish. Yes, these terrible words, 'God, why have you forsaken me?', are a verse from a psalm, but we should not draw false comfort from this. They do not necessarily mean that amid the horror of his dying Jesus is quietly reciting the Psalms as if everything is really okay.

He is really suffering, and part of that suffering is not just the physical pain, but the awful empty darkness of feeling abandoned.

The Psalms give voice to this torment. They are there for him to draw on when other words may have been impossible. They do not mean the torment is not real. Therefore, one of the hardest things to look at in the passion story is the terrible unnerving truth that in his passion and death Jesus participates in the deepest darkness of human despair and emptiness, a despair and emptiness that the Psalms do not shy away from voicing. This is where we will soon turn.

~

The first Bible I ever read was a small pocket-sized Gideons Bible, given to me in my first year at secondary school.

At the back there was an index of passages that you could read if you were feeling anxious or depressed or bereaved or resentful – or pretty much whatever you were feeling. I didn't know where to begin with reading the Bible, so I turned to the back and looked up the recommended passage for how I was feeling at the time. It didn't get me very far, but it did, I suppose, begin to navigate me towards the idea that this vast, beautiful, complex and slightly intimidating library of books had something to offer that could bring consolation and meaning to my life.

That's what Jesus was doing when he turned to Psalm 22 on the cross. That's what I was doing as a twelve-year-old boy feeling confused and depressed about life.

Jesus was reaching for Psalm 22 because, I suppose, he knew it would make sense of his suffering and even his dying. He turns to it because his whole life and his whole understanding of God had been shaped by these Hebrew Scriptures, and particularly by the Psalms, which he evidently knew by heart. I turned to whatever passage it was, because the index at the back pointed me in that direction.

I had no hinterland of knowledge.

I hadn't been brought up going to church. I had only the slenderest grasp of what the Christian story was, let alone what it meant.

But we were both doing the same thing. In the scriptures we were seeking consolation.

Thousands of people still turn to the scriptures today. Thousands of lives are shaped by the stories and poems we find there.

Thousands are discovering the Bible, sometimes through associations like the Gideons, or more probably today through an internet search or on their phone.

And I love the story (though I don't know whether it's true) of the prison inmate who used the wafer-thin pages of a New Testament as cigarette papers, read each page before he rolled his fag, and, it is said, was converted to the Christian faith by the time he got to the opening chapters of John's Gospel.

I know another story, told me by a colleague some years ago, of a young man attending church on his own several Sundays running. The vicar didn't pay him a huge amount of attention, since it seemed as if the young man always sat fairly close to an attractive young woman in the congregation and that his interest in attending church was more about her than the gospel.

But the vicar was wrong.

On the third week, when he was in church and the young woman wasn't, the vicar engaged him in conversation at the church door and the young man told him that he wanted to find out more about the Christian faith and could the vicar suggest a book for him to read?

When I first heard this story, at this point I mentally ran my eyes along my bookshelves wondering what book I would suggest to someone in such a situation. To my slight embarrassment, the book the vicar suggested was the Bible. I suppose I should have thought of that one. But, if I'm honest, and despite the consolation the Gideons Bible had brought me as an adolescent, I don't know whether I would have had the confidence just to put a Bible into the hands of someone who had not been brought up and formed in the Christian faith. Would it be just too confusing? Where should you begin?

Well, sensibly, this vicar told the young man not to start at the beginning and plough his way from Genesis onwards, but to start with one of the Gospels, maybe Mark or Luke.

The following evening, so the story goes, the young man phoned the vicar up. 'I've read it,' he said. 'I've got a few questions.'

Well, you would, wouldn't you! He hadn't actually read the whole Bible cover to cover in twenty-four hours. But he had read the New Testament. He had started at Matthew's Gospel, and just kept going.

Realising that something was happening in the heart and mind of this young man, the vicar dropped everything and arranged to meet him. He did indeed have many questions, but before he asked them he told the vicar that he had found reading the New Testament profoundly moving and profoundly challenging. He said – and these are the words I remember – 'It is the most incredible message of love.'

I find the story challenging and moving because even if I had the confidence to give a Bible to someone outside the Christian community, I'm not sure I have the confidence that in reading it they would be able to express the heart of its story with such profound simplicity: an incredible message of love.

However, that is the truth of the story, and, as we are discovering, it is a story of love that is worked out and communicated through painful suffering. Jesus is forsaken, and in his forsakenness, we find the story of God.

Another story I know to be true is of Terry Waite, the Archbishop of Canterbury's peace envoy who, while visiting Lebanon in 1987, working to secure the release of hostages, was kidnapped and became a hostage himself and then spent five long and lonely years in solitary confinement.

For three of those years he had no books and no papers. Chained to a radiator for most of the day, he experienced extreme isolation, and the torments that go with it.

I heard him talking about his experiences on the wonderful Radio 4 series *Soul Music*. Each episode focuses on a particular piece of music. There is often a little bit of history about the music's origins or something about its form and structure, but most of the programme is about how the music has touched the soul of various people.

Terry Waite was talking about how Elgar's tremendous setting of John Henry Newman's poem, *The Dream of Gerontius*, had touched his life. He explained that after four and a half years of his five-year imprisonment he was given a small battery-operated transistor radio. This was in the days when the BBC World Service still broadcast music. On the first night he had the radio they were broadcasting live from the Proms in the Albert Hall, and the orchestra were playing Elgar's famous piece. Terry Waite said that the music took him out of his captivity. Moreover, even though Newman's words are full of meaning and rich with Christian hope and consolation, particularly to those at the point of death, Terry Waite said that it was in 'the music not the words . . . that I found the harmony I needed, and was taken out of my captivity'.[2]

Might this also be what Jesus is doing in reaching for Psalm 22? Not just the words – though the words of this psalm are also full of meaning and ultimately rich with hope – but the music. Perhaps literally the music, for he remembered the song of psalmody from the synagogue. The little notes at the beginning of Psalm 22 says to the worship leader or chief musician that it is 'according to The Deer of the Dawn'. We're not really sure what this means, but it could well refer to the name of the tune, just as in our hymnals the tunes have names like *Cwm Rhondda* or *Abbots Leigh*.

So this psalm was sung, and Jesus would remember singing it. However, I'm also thinking here of the beauty of the music of God and the harmony of prayer and the hope of consolation that comes from worship, and the big picture of the gospel message: that it is indeed an incredible message of love. And how I, and the whole Church, need to have our confidence lifted so that the music and meaning of this message will prevail and will endure. It will help people find identity and purpose, even in the midst of great suffering.

When we worship, and especially when we worship together, or even when we are joining in via a crackly radio chained to a radiator in a tiny cell a thousand miles away, or when we are strung up on a cross, mocked and ridiculed by a cackling crowd, we are taken out of ourselves. We are taken into something bigger than ourselves.

It is the first step in the reconfiguring of our humanity, no longer putting ourselves at the centre of the universe, but joining in solidarity with a great company of believers, both the Church on earth with all its shortcomings and misgivings, *and* the Church in heaven, the angels and archangels, cherubim and seraphim, and finding that we at last become who we are meant to be.

'I worship, therefore I am' is the Christian response to the utilitarian philosophies of the world.[3]

William Temple, one of my greatest predecessors, famously said, that 'to worship is to quicken the conscience by the holiness of God, to feed the mind with the truth of God, to purge the imagination by the beauty of God, to open the heart to the love of God, to devote the will to the purpose of God'.[4]

Amazingly, and despite its horrors, we worship at the cross. At the cross we see God's love and the beauty and depths of God's love in painful detail.

George Herbert's famous poem 'Prayer' is really just a list of phrases, each one a profound definition of prayer and capable of becoming the opening line of a poem or an essay on that aspect of prayer, but none able to carry the weight and meaning of prayer on its own. Three phrases in particular stand out for me as I think of Jesus crying out on the cross. Herbert says in the opening line that prayer is 'A kind of banquet.' He ends by saying, 'It is something understood.' In the middle he says, 'It is a kind of tune.'[5]

When I have nothing to say. When prayer eludes me. When faith is hopelessly small. When life is wretched. When I face persecution and death itself, there are words available to me to give my longings voice and substance. They are the words of scripture. Words I can reach for. Words I may begin to teach myself, for it is never too late to learn a single phrase. It is a banquet I return to. An understanding that comes from standing under. A kind of tune. It feeds my mind and imagination. It opens my heart.

I am not left behind. I am not forgotten. Someone who has been forsaken like me – even godforsaken like me – and who knows what it feels like to be abandoned and alone, has come back for me. His words can be mine.

Questions

1. Are there other bits of scripture outside the Gospels themselves that help you to understand the cross?
2. When did you first read the Bible? What did you make of it? How is it part of your Christian life today?
3. What does it mean to you to speak of 'worshipping at the cross'?
4. Do you have any stories or experiences of how people have come to faith or found strength through the cross?

FOUR

When Jesus cried out 'Eloi, Eloi, lema sabachthani' the people standing at the foot of the cross misunderstood him.

They didn't speak Aramaic. Or they didn't hear him correctly. Or they weren't really that interested. Whatever the reason, they didn't know or recognise these words as the beginning of a long recital of Psalm 22 or even just a quotation from the opening line, still less the aching cry of dereliction that we know them to be through the translations we have received. It's not that they were horrified by Jesus' anguish, nor comforted by his reliance on scripture: they had no idea what he was on about.

It is, in so many respects, one of the most painful details of the story. Jesus utters these monumental words, wrenched and wrung out from the heart of suffering – a recitation – but no one understands him.

This is worse than being ignored. They don't just shrug their shoulders at their miscomprehension. They actually get him wrong. They mistranslate him. The bystanders hear the Aramaic word 'Eloi' – 'my Lord' – and think he's saying 'Elijah'. 'Listen,' they cry in Mark's Gospel, 'he is calling for Elijah' (Mark 15.35). And in Matthew's Gospel they go further, saying, 'Wait, let us see whether Elijah will come to save him' (Matthew 27.49).

This is an additional indignity. Enjoying the spectacle of death, they peevishly speculate that there might be even more excitement to come. But they don't hear what he is really saying.

Isn't this the whole, terrible tragedy of Jesus' ministry? Even at the last, even in his death, even as he utters his final words, he is misunderstood. People don't know him. People don't understand what he is saying. People get him wrong; even those who claim to know him best.

As we come to the cross and try to hear what Jesus is saying and what it means, we can't help notice that most of those who had been following him and who promised they would endure with him to the end have fled. This is the painful trajectory of the story: one by one, those who thought they knew him find out they don't. They misunderstand him. They abandon him. They even betray him. They pretend they never even knew him. Either wilfully or unwittingly, they get his words wrong. As we do, too. They mistranslate him.

Jesus cries out that he's forsaken by God, but he's pretty much forsaken by everyone else as well. They get him wrong.

This is also something of a theme in Mark's Gospel, sometimes referred to as *secrecy*.

In Mark's Gospel when Jesus heals people he asks them not to tell anyone what has happened.

A leper who is healed is sternly warned to 'say nothing to anyone' about what has happened (Mark 1.44). The deaf man whose hearing is restored, and those who witnessed it, are ordered 'to tell no one' (Mark 7.36).

But this isn't really feasible. Mark observes that the man healed from leprosy 'went out and began to proclaim it freely' (Mark 1.45), and as for the deaf man and his friends, 'the more he ordered them, the more zealously they proclaimed it' (Mark 7.36). And, anyway, if you had leprosy and now you don't, or if you were deaf and now you can hear, how are you supposed to keep it a secret!

A cynical response to all this might be that of course the very best way to ensure fickle and unreliable human beings spread a message is to swear them to secrecy! They are then bound to share it. However, I think something else is going on here in Mark's rich and beautiful narrative.

As we have already noted, the Gospel begins with a clear declaration that this is the story of Jesus, the Son of God. No secrecy here. However, as the Gospel unfolds, only the demons and those on the edge of the story who have little agency or power seem to know who Jesus is. Crying out from a possessed man, the demons who are legion scream in protest at his power over them: 'What have you to do with me, Jesus, Son of the Most High God?' they cry (Mark 5.7). They alone address him by his correct title!

Likewise, there are others whose illness or lack of status has separated them from everyone else who reach out to Jesus with simple confidence and faith.

Like the man with leprosy, intuitively recognising who Jesus is, and saying to him, 'If you choose, you can make me clean' (Mark 1.40).

Or blind Bartimaeus, stubbornly calling out for mercy, even when the disciples try to shut him up.

Or the Gentile woman whose persistence outwits Jesus, and whose faithfulness shames those who claim to know him (see Mark 7.24–30).

Or the little children whom the disciples again try and turn away, but whom Jesus blesses and commends as those who belong to his kingdom (see Mark 10.13–16).

Mark is putting the forsaken at the centre of the story. The little people. The lost. Those who are excluded because of race, religion, ethnicity, illness and what is deemed unclean and unworthy. The one who has such a heart of love and was so moved with pity for those who were forsaken will himself become forsaken, unrecognised, unheard and misunderstood: he will, upon the cross, become the one who is abandoned. It is so important to understand this. The forsaken, and even the godforsaken, are at the centre of the story, the lowly who will be lifted high, and it is most obviously for them that Jesus is becoming forsaken himself.

Moreover, and because of this, Mark is constantly leading us to the cross. This is the heart of the story, Jesus' 'at-one-ness' with those who are lost. Mark doesn't want us to settle for anything less. Yes, Jesus is an amazing miracle worker and a wonderful teacher. But this is not the whole story. In him, God is made visible in an astonishing way. But the secrecy isn't that Jesus is the Messiah. That is obvious, it is where Mark begins, and the healings emphasise his sovereignty and power, giving his teaching an authenticity and integrity that no one has ever experienced before, even if it is only the demons and those in great need who understand it. No, the secret is much more *what sort of Messiah he will be.* It is not going to be as anyone expects. Especially not the religious experts.

So when Peter does, at last, and over halfway through the story, recognise who Jesus is, and declares him as Messiah, Jesus not only forbids him to tell anyone (Mark 8.29–30) but then goes on to speak about his death and resurrection (Mark 8.31). He is trying to tell Peter what sort of Messiah he will be. But Peter can't take it. A few moments earlier he had spoken with incredible insight; now he rails against Jesus and is rebuked.

This will be a pattern for Peter. As he gets things right, so he also gets things wrong. For him, as for virtually all of Jesus' followers, it will only be after the resurrection that he's able to piece the story together properly and understand who Jesus is.

Jesus gives them loads of clues. He predicts his passion and death at least three times. His stories, not least the one he tells of wicked tenants who seize the vineyard they are farming and kill the son and heir (see Mark 12.1–11), point towards the terrible truth that it will be through his dying and his forsakenness that the scripture will be fulfilled that 'the stone that the builders rejected has become the cornerstone' (Mark 12.10 and Psalm 118.22). But they don't get it. Or, perhaps, they don't *want* to get it. Like us they are too busy creating God in their own image, or arguing over who is the greatest. And a God who suffers, a God who is forsaken, is difficult to understand.

Finally, in another poignantly painful point in the story, Peter – the one who had promised that when everyone else failed he would stand firm – denies he ever even knew Jesus. After Jesus' arrest, and with him following at a distance, a servant girl challenges him, asking whether he is a follower of Jesus. 'I don't even know that man!' Peter replies (Luke 22.57, CEV). It turns out to be the truest thing he ever said.

Isn't this also true for us? Jesus dies, as he lived, with people not getting him. His words are mis-heard and misunderstood, and, sadly, this has not changed much. Wilfully, mistakenly, foolishly or purposefully, because of cowardice and neglect, we get Jesus wrong.

We hear what we want to hear. We do what we want to do. We pray for what we want to get.

We get faith wrong. We think of it as a ticket to heaven rather than a blueprint for life. We are timid, when we should be bold; polite, when we should be filled with righteous anger; focused on ourselves, when we should be focused on God and upon God's kingdom.

We pick and choose. We sift and edit. We discard the uncomfortable bits of Christian faith; and especially the cross and the discomfort of Jesus' wretched forsakenness.

We make the Christian faith fit. Or wait for a miracle. Perhaps still thinking that Elijah might come and take him down, and give us a different story and a different God.

This might be the nub of it: we don't change ourselves, we want God to change. If only God were a bit more like us. '*Thy* will be done' gradually becomes '*my* will be done'.

Isn't this the terrible, startling truth of it? God is like us because God has become *forsaken like us*. It's just that we have shut ourselves away from this forsakenness, especially in a society like ours, where, even with Covid, we are able to pretend that we might live for ever. We don't talk about death and dying very much. We've lost the rituals and customs that helped us through bereavement. We even view talk about age and ageing as if it is some sort of failure. We certainly do all that we can to remain youthful for as long as possible and to hide, disguise or even surgically remove the effects of ageing. None of this is necessarily wrong, but it can be dangerous and prevent us from facing the ultimate reality of our living: that is, that we will die.

And isn't this why Jesus died? Because that is what human beings do – we die. *And Jesus has become a messiah who is completely human. Because we couldn't save ourselves.* Because we get things wrong. Because we cherish the illusion that death might leave us alone.

It is this salvation, wrought in the very heart of how and where we get it wrong, that is the central meaning of the Christian faith: that Jesus came to save sinners – that is, forsaken people – including those who don't know they're forsaken and who pretend otherwise, and who have avoided thinking about the loneliness of death. In Christ, God is making it right for those who get it wrong.

That's what we hear on the cross as Jesus cries out, 'Why have you abandoned me?' It is a discovery of how little we know; a timely encounter with our lack of understanding: face to face in the face of Jesus as he dies. It is the unmasking of illusion. A liberating shot of reality.

~

Like most priests, I have sat at many deathbeds and had many conversations with people approaching death. Most of them have not been particularly profound. The deathbed itself is usually a place of attentive vigil; of holding and remembering; of simple prayer. But not a lot of conversation. Loved ones, taking it in turns to watch and wait, will often talk with each other. But, usually, the dying person is slipping away from life and therefore away from the chatter of human discourse.

The really important communication continues through touch. We hold a loved one's hand. We kiss their brow. And even the priest – in the end – though reciting the powerfully comfortable words of the liturgy, knows it is the actions that speak more clearly: the last Holy Communion; the grease of chrism; the sign of the cross.

This is also true of Jesus' death. A few people – in Mark's Gospel, just the women – stand in patient watchfulness. They don't say much. Even Jesus only says the astonishing words that we are addressing. The important thing is the death itself. And those of us who aren't dying yet must watch and wait.

Julian of Norwich, on what everyone thought was her deathbed in 1373, aged thirty, was given the last rites. A crucifix was held before her eyes. And as she looked, she received fourteen 'shewings' of the love of God through the passion and death of Christ. I love that Old English word 'shewing'. We've translated it 'revelation'. But I like the simpler, more straightforward sense of God *showing her something* through the death of Christ and through what she thought to be her own death. When, to everyone's amazement, she got better she wrote these shewings down. They are one of the most incredible and beautiful records of what happens in us as we look at the cross and stand under it.

I remember one conversation I had with a priest I served when I was Bishop of Chelmsford. He died in 2014. His name was Chris, and he was a team vicar at Great Chesterford, near Saffron Walden. Still a relatively young man in his late fifties, as I remember, cancer just gnawed away at him. I went to see him a couple of times and on one occasion, a few months before he actually died, we had a profoundly beautiful conversation. In it, he showed me something.

He told me in an admirably straightforward and good-humoured manner, which got alarmingly to the heart of things, about his faithful friends and the well-intentioned comfort they offered him. He told me that his High Church friends wanted to take him to Walsingham or Lourdes to be healed. And his

Low Church friends wanted to take him to some charismatic bash or to a Christian Healing Centre. But he, Chris, wanted none of it. He told me that, of course, he wanted to be healed. He wanted life to go on and felt angry that it was being taken away before what he considered to be his allotted time. He told me he was scared sometimes, and ached with the bitter knowledge that he would not see his children's future. But he also told me, he had arrived at a place – or should I say God had led him to a place – where he had come to know that healing no longer meant getting better in the sense that the cancer would go away. It was something else. It wasn't that he'd stopped believing that God could do such a thing; he, like many of us, had witnessed the inexplicable, where other people facing similar illnesses had got better, and prayed for it fervently. It was just that he knew, and that God had led him to a place of knowing, which was the other side of such accounts of healing, that health, in the fullest Christian understanding of the word, meant salvation. It wasn't simply a condition of the body, but the readiness of the mind and heart and strength and will to *know God* and to be *in Christ*, the Christ who is with us in his suffering and death, and *with Christ* to cleave to the Father.

And here I might want to say, and pray with Christ, 'Into your hands I place my spirit.' As we discovered earlier, these are the words that many have prayed and made their own on their deathbed. But it wasn't as straightforward as this for Chris.

At that point, still a few months away from death, and still able to do things and hold conversations, he had also come to know it was about living with the steady demise of his body and the ravages of the cancer, and therefore would also mean very human howls of outrage against God; this too was part of preparing for death.

Consequently, he also told me that, paradoxically, his prayer was shot through with a tremendous thanksgiving in ways he had never known before. And here we might note that the last ten verses of Psalm 22 are all thanksgiving. The one who has been so afflicted and tormented, now cries out, 'You who fear the Lord, praise him . . . stand in awe of him' (Psalm 22.23). And, indeed, 'all who sleep in the earth . . . who go down to the dust . . . shall live for him' (Psalm 22.29).

Chris was saying to me that it wasn't so much that he didn't know what to pray for if he wasn't going to go to Lourdes or Walsingham; it was that he had been overtaken by an incredible awareness that he had *never known what to pray for*, that he had always been getting prayer wrong, and, perhaps, like most of us, always been in danger of seeing prayer as asking God for stuff, that God might rearrange the universe for our convenience, and, therefore, he had got faith wrong. When death was just a point on the distant horizon of his life he could pray differently, because life still held choice and opportunity and he still had agency. But now those choices were steadily diminishing, even the choice or opportunity that he might get better. And even if he did get better, was this really the thing to pray for, since it only meant postponing the real challenge of prayer, which was not to ask God for things, even length of days, but to *thank God for what is and what will be*, for without God there is nothing, and because of God, that is God in Christ participating in the sorrow and suffering of the world, there was the hope that this universe itself in all its complex but fallible beauty, and he a part of it, would be made new.

And so paradoxically, and with the knowledge of approaching death, his heart was thankful. Thankful for the gift of each day. Thankful for the tremendous love and support of his wife and boys. Thankful for the hundreds of little acts of kindness he received. Thankful for the faith that was carrying him to something beyond, even if this also meant anger and frustration that this was neither the way nor the time he would have chosen. In fact, it was this emptying out of all that he thought he knew about God and faith and prayer and the brutal honesty of his anger before God that had led him to thankfulness. He had found that this would either destroy his faith, or lead him to a faith of utter simplicity, just him standing before the cross and knowing that God in Christ had gone this way before him. In this radical simplicity, prayer was, for him, at last becoming something understood.

A couple of years after Chris died, I was asked to write a prayer that would go on tube trains in London and Newcastle. Using advertising space on public transport networks, it was part of a national campaign called *Prayers on the Move* aimed at encouraging people, of all faiths and none, to think about and engage in prayer in a challenging but accessible way. Each prayer could only be a sentence or two. I enjoyed the challenge. This is what I wrote: 'My heart, it still keeps beating. But what for? Show me how to measure my life in something other than years.'

Questions

1. Where do you think you might have got Jesus wrong?
2. What do you find most difficult to understand about the Christian faith?
3. What do you pray for? And what is the deepest longing of your heart?
4. How do you think prayer might change if you always imagined you were saying your prayers standing at the foot of the cross? Or even on your deathbed?

FIVE

The words that Jesus cries out as he dies
are terrifying: *My God, my God,
why have you forsaken me?*

We recoil from them. They challenge our understanding of Jesus and they challenge our understanding of the cross. They stir the pot of our darkest anxieties. They correspond too closely to our own experience of sometimes feeling abandoned by God in times of deep need or isolating pain. We shudder with dread.

Yes, in some senses we can hear them as words of hope: as we have seen, in their context in Psalm 22 they begin to map out a theological commentary on the passion and as such were drawn on by the early Church when it told the story of the cross.

It is also comforting to see that Jesus knows what it is to be human, that he plumbed the deepest depths of abandonment and despair.

Nevertheless, however much we comfort ourselves with these thoughts, we cannot avoid the stark and formidable reality of the words themselves. As well as a source of hope, they are a sticking point of despair. If this was Jesus' experience, how can we call the cross a victory? How can it be the source of salvation? How – and this is the really chilling conclusion – amid all the ongoing horrors and the colossal pain in the world, can the cross be anything other than a brutal reaffirmation that it is a cruel and ugly place, that the innocent suffer, and that God, if God does exist, has either lost control or doesn't care?

That is why the Church down the centuries, as I have done in this book, keeps reminding everyone that the words are from the Psalms; it is why the New Testament insists that the death and resurrection of Jesus happens in accordance with scripture.

And yet the truth is that as we hear them we are much closer to the taunting crowds than we are to Jesus. Because we want to shout out, as they did: 'Save yourself if you are the Son of God. Show your power' (see Mark 15.30). Maybe – and this is a very hard thought – out of the sheer bloody hopelessness of it all, we want to jeer as well. And the fact that Mark has Jesus crying out in desolation with these terrible words (and none of the more comforting ones we find in the other Gospels), knowing they will be a stumbling block for many, fuels this anxiety and fuels our despair.

This is because we really want a different sort of Jesus. Not one that suffers. Not one who is so agonisingly human. This Jesus is too like the despairing person we are ourselves.

Philip Larkin famously and also despairingly described religion as 'that vast moth-eaten musical brocade / created to pretend we never die'.[1] When we hear Jesus saying that he is forsaken, even those of us who place our trust in God, but who are still, of course, fearful of death, doubt the comforts and creeds of our faith as we move inexorably towards our own death, what Larkin also calls in the same desolate poem, 'the sure extinction that we travel to . . . nothing more terrible, nothing more true'.[2]

No, we want a Jesus who is in control.

We like him when he is casting out demons and blessing small children. We like him when he is healing the sick. We like him when he rebukes the powerful and tells his beautiful stories. But we are nervous and uncertain when we find Jesus saying the very things we say; when we hear him cry out to God in the same anguish and abandonment we know so well.

The words *'lema sabachthani'* mean 'Why have you left me alone?' That is the overcasting horror of them. Crucifixion, we know, is a most horrifying, drawn-out and painful way to die. Jesus is in immense physical pain. We know this. It is ghastly enough. But now it seems he is in spiritual torment as well.

Lema sabachthani is the agonised cry of one who has been abandoned; one who has been deserted by the one they love and the one they thought loved them. The pain is not just the pain of isolation. It is much, much worse. It is the pain of being left alone. The one I love and need was with me. Now they have gone. I thought they loved me. I thought this love was for ever. Now it is just me. Love itself has left me behind. This is how it was for Jesus.

Hearing anyone say such words is painful, but to hear them on the lips of Jesus is impossibly so. The one who has left Jesus behind is God the Father. God had the power to stay with Jesus, but God has chosen not to. And even if they are a quote from Psalm 22, doesn't this just mean that someone else was once as anguished as Jesus was and he is borrowing their terrible words? It certainly can't just mean that amid the horror of his dying Jesus is quietly reciting the Psalms and really everything is okay.

Throughout his ministry Jesus tells us that he is one with God. To Philip he says, 'Whoever has seen me has seen the Father' (John 14.9). But where is that 'oneness' now?

Sometimes well-meaning Christian ministers, and even perhaps one or two theologians, get round this difficulty not just by reference to Psalm 22, but by saying that Jesus only suffered *in his humanity*, not in his divinity. At one level, this sounds helpful. But it is too neat. Jesus is fully God *and* fully human. This is the basic Christian declaration about the person of Christ; that in him our frail, corruptible and mortal flesh is united with the everlasting, incorruptible and uncreated, eternal life of God. The divine and human natures of Jesus do not exist beside one another. His humanity and divinity are indivisible. They are joined in him in a personal unity. The Nicene Creed, which agreed the boundary markers around this vital Christian doctrine against those heresies that either said Jesus was some sort of superman who became God, or was never really fully human at all, but God, as it were, in the disguise of human flesh, speaks of Jesus as 'being of one substance with the Father ... and who was incarnate – made flesh – from the Holy Spirit and the Virgin Mary'.[3]

Jesus is therefore nothing less than God; and he is nothing less than human. Moreover, this great Christian truth is either true all the time, or not true at all. We cannot therefore untangle the painful difficulty of Jesus crying out that he is forsaken by God, by separating out his two natures whenever some unpleasantness – or theological difficulty – comes along as if he suffered in his humanity – his flesh – but not in his divinity; as if somehow in his spirit or inner being (whatever that is!) he was simply waiting patiently for it to be over. Jesus was a totality of mind, body and spirit, like us because he was fully human, and he was also, without ever relinquishing what it is to be fully human, fully God.

Luke and John, as we have mentioned, solve the problem by omitting Jesus' words of forsakenness from their accounts, but this does not mean they leave out Christ's suffering; they re-emphasise it, so as to focus on the triumph of the cross, in John's case; and in Luke, on Christ's gentleness, forbearance and innocence.

Moreover, can these words say anything to our experiences of being bewildered and abandoned?

Nowadays, many people are turned away from the Christian faith because they either don't understand why it is that Jesus had to suffer and die (it seems to make God a rather cruel and vindictive father). Or they cannot love a God who calls himself love yet appears to permit such terrible suffering in the world, and here even in his own Son. Certainly, the weight of evidence seems to be against God.

There is so much suffering in our world. So much that is wrong. Millions starve. Children are without fresh water. A cyclone devastates a coastal community. Rainforests disappear. Cheap burgers remain cheap and are available everywhere.

Ancient ways of life disappear. The balance and equilibrium of the planet itself are undermined. An earthquake erupts and thousands die. Sea levels rise. Forest fires rage. Instability breeds despair and outrage. Extremism flourishes in the fertile ground of fake news. The vitriolic echo chambers of social media hum with delight at other people's foibles and failings. The brutal certainties of the self-righteous stamp out nuance and suffocate perspective. Everyone has their own truth. A terrorist steps into a mosque with the dates of Christian Crusades initialled into the handle of his automatic weapon. A few nations get an upgrade to their vast arsenals of nuclear weapons. Hundreds of others call for their removal. A few vie for a place at the nuclear top table themselves.

Even in our own country, one of the wealthiest in the world, a widening gap between rich and poor means life expectancy levels for some are massively higher than for others. Some enjoy easy access to care and education. Others don't. At so-called 'conventional arms fairs', sophisticated weapons exchange hands for large sums of money. Our pension funds swell. There are smiles all round. Meanwhile in other parts of the world oppressed people end up more oppressed. Tanks cross borders. Desperate people flee for their lives or mount an insurrection with homemade bombs. Back home the overseas aid budget is cut. Racial intolerance festers. Ungodly privileges for a protected elite flourish. Lack of resources for education and health, poor and inadequate housing, wilfully stunted ambition mean whole generations and whole communities feel left behind, forsaken. The breakdown of the norms and standards that govern public life means that even those who lead us are seen to get away with lies. They rule with bluster and deceit, and no one has faith in anything any more, believing everyone is just out for themselves, that truth really is a matter of personal choice.

Where is God? we say. How can God be justified?

The crowds say to Jesus: 'Save yourself' (Mark 15.30). And

in Matthew's Gospel, even more pointedly: 'If you are the Son of God, come down from the cross' (Matthew 27.40).

We read the story today, we hear Jesus crying out in desperation, and think they have a point. Our objections and concerns are not a million miles away from their sneers. If God is as God says he is, why doesn't he intervene? If Jesus has the power that we have seen demonstrated elsewhere in the story, why doesn't he save himself? Don't these words of dereliction prove either God's helplessness, or that the whole thing really is a tragic charade, the moth-eaten musical brocade that Larkin spoke of?

Moreover, however much we try to explain these words away, shouldn't we also face the horror that maybe at the last, in those final agonising moments, Jesus himself stopped believing in God, stopped reckoning himself the Messiah, was utterly defeated and abandoned. Isn't this what the words actually mean?

The cross is real. It is horribly real. It is real horror and real pain. Jesus is really suffering, and part of that suffering is not just the physical pain, but the awful empty darkness of feeling abandoned. The Psalms give voice to his torment: they are there for him to draw on when other words may have been almost impossible, but they do not mean the torment is unreal. Therefore, one of the hardest things to look at in the passion story – the thing we are most likely to shy away from, and probably the reason why so many Christian people don't turn up to church on Good Friday – is the terrible, unnerving truth that in his passion and death Jesus participates in the deepest darkness of human despair and emptiness: Jesus, the one whom we understand to be God's Son, hangs dying on the cross and he feels as abandoned by God as we do sometimes. Perhaps, more so.

So if this is how Jesus feels, we may ask, how can we ever expect to feel anything other than abandonment ourselves? How can we find help when we feel bewildered and forsaken? And today, when so many people are turned away from the Christian faith by a conviction that a God who seems to allow such suffering in the world – and even the suffering of his own Son – is not worthy of worship, these words simply reinforce a humanistic view of Jesus: he was a good man, but not God; one who in the end shared our dereliction. But there is nothing else to life. Larkin was right, and death is the last, brutal full stop.

That's what Jesus experienced and that's what I will experience. 'This is the anaesthetic from which no one comes round', as Larkin put it.[4]

~

As I was going about the final edit of this book, I visited the retrospective exhibition of Francis Bacon's paintings at the Royal Academy. The exhibition was entitled *Man and Beast*. This is a recurring theme in Bacon's bleak and godless renditions of humanity: the veil is lifted on our so-called sophisticated, tamed and civilised selves and a glowering, furious bestial amorality is revealed. In each painting, a tortured and distorted, barely human being cowers in defeated fear or screams in furious agony. Sometimes the animals before us are some sort of contorted hybrid creature, neither entirely man nor beast. Yet their rage, fear and submission to pain and fate feel very human indeed. It is like staring into the jaws of hell. Though even this isn't quite accurate, for hell at least carries with it the possibility of heaven somewhere. These paintings stare into the abyss of annihilation and empty and eternal forsakenness.

Is this our greatest fear? That we really are just brute beasts, with nothing beyond us and a simmering, barely controlled violence within us?

Each painting also contains lines and boundaries. The person or animal in the frame appear as if a specimen in a jar.

Are we being invited to examine ourselves as we really are, as we might be? 'We are meat,' said Francis Bacon. 'We are all potential carcasses.'[5]

Bacon is undoubtedly one of the most important painters of the twentieth century. His life spanned most of that troubled era. Perhaps it took Passchendaele, Auschwitz, Hiroshima, the killing fields of Cambodia and all the cruel certainties that fuelled them and the horrors we did to each other to produce such terrible, terrifying images of defeated, forsaken humanity.

Bacon's first acclaimed painting in 1933 was of the crucifixion. It was also the first painting in the exhibition at the Royal Academy. In the next room were the paintings that made his name: three bestial figures crawling menacingly around the foot of the cross. But the cross held no religious significance for Bacon. He had no religious belief that we know of. He viewed the cross as 'just an act of man's behaviour'.[6] He saw there not innocent or heroic suffering, but calculated cruelty and random, spiteful violence. His ghostly, skeletal Christ foreshadows all the rest of his output declaring that human beings are fundamentally animals. And nothing more.

This is where we are left: frightened, defeated, abandoned, alone. It seems as if life has no meaning beyond that which we impose upon it, or draw from it, in the fleeting moments of our days. So human love is still real and still beautiful. Kindness still matters. But there is no ultimate meaning. Strip away the veneer of our civilisation and we are brute beasts who will tear each other apart. In addition, the cross of Jesus whom some called the Christ is just the most terrible example of this. Not just because crucifixion was such a ghastly way of killing people, but because this Jesus was such a wonderfully good man, even, we might say, blessed by God. But he ends up the same as the rest of us – frightened, defeated, abandoned, alone. This cruelty isn't even just the random cruelty of an earthquake or a virus, but the deliberate and pitiless killing of one human being by another, and therefore it also demonstrates our terrible capacity to, as Rachel Mann has put it, 'suspend our capacity to suffer with'[7] someone. 'It reveals how the most significant friendships and relationships can end up in the wreckage of betrayal, failure, denial and cowardice.'[8]

To be part of the execution of this horror you have to render yourself less than human. You have to refuse to see the humanity of another. You have to submit to that bestial fury that I suppose we know is inside us, but is, for the most part, under control. Unleashed, there is a devouring rage that can and does consume everything, including ourselves and our humanity. It is a terrible cycle of demeaning violence. We learn to hate. We learn to destroy. We learn to kill and not to care. And, as we also know, those who have been exploited and abused sometimes end up exploiting and abusing others. Not all. Many, amazingly, rise above it. However, they too, die. That is the bottom line, the rock-bottom line of despair that Jesus' words, and even more than the words, the howl of agony that goes with them, encapsulate.

Moreover, in my ministry as a priest I have sat with many people in such agony, people who felt abandoned, or who were gripped by the chill fear of death, or were hurting, or have been the victims of violence and abuse. I have also met perpetrators of terrible crimes who have been overwhelmed by this fury, all but destroyed by it, eaten out by an inner cancer of deceitful and consuming rage, and don't know where to go or where to turn.

All this is horribly captured in Francis Bacon's paintings, who at the same time, perhaps even more alarmingly, captures the inner howls of despair that lie beneath the ordinary veneer of so-called ordinary lives, the terrors and agonies that are within. But also, if we're honest, they are held in the words of Jesus when we just take them as they are. No amount of clever explaining away eliminates or reduces the stupefying horror that maybe in those final agonising moments Jesus himself stopped believing in God, stopped reckoning himself the Messiah, was utterly defeated and abandoned. Isn't this what the words actually mean?

Or is it?

Is there something else?

Questions

1. What are the things happening in the world, or even in your own life at the moment if you feel able to share them, that cause you horror and challenge your belief in God?
2. Have there been times when your faith has been stretched to the limit, or even broken, by the sadness and suffering of the world? And what brought you back to faith?
3. Does being a Christian change the way you understand and approach these things. If so, how?
4. How does a Christian faith with a cross at the centre change the way you think about God?

SIX

As Jesus dies on the cross, Mark tells us
there was darkness over the land (Mark 15.33).

Jesus' words come from the heart of darkness and are spoken into a world of darkness. They are dark words. They take us to the heart of our own darkness and despair. They plumb the depths of darkness, or as the Apostles' Creed puts it, explaining the deepest, darkest meaning of Jesus' death: 'He descended into hell.'[1]

He cries out: 'My God, my God, why have you forsaken me?' The crowds misunderstand him as usual. Most of his followers have fled. But after the crowds wait to see if Elijah will come and save him, Mark tells us that Jesus gave *another loud cry* and then breathed his last (Mark 15.37).

There are no words this time. Just a cry. Just, we suppose, a howl of sorrow and of pain. Then he dies.

The darkness persists. It seems as if it has triumphed.

Then Mark says this: 'The curtain of the temple was torn in two, from top to bottom' (Mark 15.38) and that 'when the centurion, who stood facing him' – presumably one of those who had nailed him there in the first place and is now standing guard – 'saw that in this way he breathed his last, he said, "Truly this man was God's Son!"' (Mark 15.39).

As we explored earlier, in St Mark's Gospel Jesus is, at first, a secretive figure, a man of action who commands silence from those he heals. The secret that Mark's Gospel reveals is not that Jesus is the Messiah (as we have already observed, that is stated plainly in the opening sentence of the book), but the *nature of his messiahship*: Mark tells us that Jesus is a Messiah who must suffer and die.

Those who followed Jesus found this message difficult to swallow.

Judas maybe betrays Jesus because he can't understand this intellectually. He wanted Jesus to bring in the kingdom.

Peter denies Jesus because he can't understand this emotionally. He liked walking on water. He wasn't so good at sinking.

James and John simply argue about who is the greatest and who will have the best seats when Jesus establishes his kingdom.

Only the centurion standing at the foot of the cross recognises what is happening, that the death of Jesus itself, not his teaching, not his miracles, *but his dying* is the manifestation of God's love and the sure sign of God's passionate commitment to the world. 'Truly', he says, 'this man was God's Son!'

The Greek in which Mark wrote these words is not entirely straightforward to translate at this point. There is no definite or indefinite article, so some translations have the centurion saying, 'Truly this man is *the* Son of God', and others, 'Truly this man is *a* son of God.' Clearly, this offers rather different slants on the words. The NRSV translation, which I have used, gets round this by just saying 'God's Son'. But this does seem to me to be what Mark intends. The centurion's confession of faith in Jesus as *Son of God* comes about not just in stark contrast to the failings of virtually everyone else in the story, but on the basis of Jesus' death alone; and nothing else. It also leaves us with the question: is Jesus *the* Son of God? In which case how do we make sense of his suffering, his feeling abandoned by God, and his death? Or is he *a* son of God, a supremely wonderful, holy and inspiring person, but no more than that, and in the end, abandoned to death like the rest of us?

It is the question we face every time we look at the cross, every time we hear the story of Christ's passion, and every time we go to church on Good Friday: how, amid all this pain and horror, can we make such a confession of faith ourselves? How is Jesus *the* Son of God? Or, might we say, how can we still believe in him as *the* Son of God when we hear him in such devastating agony and such bewildering lostness? How can we reconcile Jesus' experience of feeling deserted by God with our conviction, as Christians, that the cross is our salvation?

Paradoxically, to do this, we are going to have to go deeper still into the words themselves; not just what they meant for Jesus, but what *they meant for God*. And we must begin by thinking about what we mean when we say the word 'God'.

As Christians, we believe in God who is Father, Son and Holy Spirit, what we call the Trinity. God is *three* persons, and *one* God.

This belief did not come out of thin air. It arose as the very first Christians reflected on their experience of Jesus, who they came to believe was completely God while still being completely human; and then their experience of the Spirit of Jesus, which was for them also the complete presence of Jesus with them, but unconstrained by time and place.

The story of Jesus in the New Testament is, then, the story of the Son of the Father, and the story of the sending and indwelling of the Spirit.

Repeatedly in John's Gospel, and to the irritation of those who consider this blasphemy, Jesus insists that he and the Father are one (see John 17.11). Yet in the events of Holy Week this 'at-one-ness' is stretched to breaking point. Jesus' desperate request in Gethsemane that there might be another way is not granted. Jesus struggles to know and be conformed to God's will. There is a contradiction. The Father and the Son are one, but Jesus concludes: 'not what I want, but what you want' (Mark 14.36). That is, at this point in the narrative, the Father and the Son want different things.

Jesus submits to the Father, prays that God's will be done in him, but it is with great dread and foreboding.

In the passion itself, this is exacerbated. Their wills appear to be divided. The Father appears to withdraw. Therefore, Jesus' cry of dereliction, 'My God, my God, why have you forsaken me?', means exactly what it says. The Son *is* forsaken by the Father. Or to make the same point in a slightly different way, but in order to emphasise what is happening to God: God is forsaken by God. There is, if we can even begin to imagine such a thing, a kind of breakdown in the very life of the Trinity. The Father forsakes the Son and in so doing the Son not only loses his sonship, but the Father loses his fatherhood. If this is the case, then what happens on Calvary (the Latin translation of Golgotha, the place of the skull), reaches into the innermost depths of God, leaving its impress in the life of the Trinity for eternity.

And this is a *necessary* breakdown. Still terrible to consider, but the inevitable consequence of what begins in the Incarnation – God's emptying of what it is to be God in order to know what it is to be human – finds its painful ending on the cross. Jesus is sharing completely in what it is to be human, and therefore sharing our forsakenness. Sharing our desolation. Sharing the dark chill of fear, which is our existential dread and our actual experience of being undone, defeated and abandoned. 'We have one who in every respect has been tested as we are, yet without sin' (Hebrews 4.15) is the way the letter to the Hebrews describes Jesus. But it also affects the very life of God. God the Father is not looking on dispassionately. Not merely waiting for it to be over. Not already basking in any anticipated glory of the happy ending that is around the corner. But really involved in the pain of this separation.

Therefore, we can conclude that Jesus was bound to plumb the depths of despair and mental anguish, the real despair of being deserted by God, as well as the physical suffering of crucifixion. He had to suffer and die. Isn't this, in fact, what he kept telling his disciples, even though – because he was human – he couldn't know exactly what it meant, nor the torment that awaited him.

In Mark's Gospel, Jesus predicts his suffering and death three times. And each time the disciples don't get it and rail against him.

On the Emmaus Road on the first Easter Day, he says to Cleopas and his companion, 'Was it not necessary that the Messiah should suffer these things and then enter into his glory?' (Luke 24.26).

In this regard, the physical suffering, terrible though it was, is overshadowed by the far greater spiritual and mental torment. But it is also, amazingly, the greatest sign that God is indeed, completely sharing what it is to be human. And even if we have heard these dreadful words, and been able to find some hope in them, because this is indeed a very human voice and an all too human response, what we may not have done is consider how God the Father is also abandoned, and dare we say it, also suffering?

Where we go wrong in our thinking – and probably in our praying as well – is to think of Jesus and God the Father *separately*. And perhaps not to think of the Holy Spirit very much at all. But when we think of God we should always think of the Trinity, the God who is Father, Son and Holy Spirit, the mysterious and beautiful life of God in the constant giving and receiving of relationship, a relationship that by this apparent separation – I don't know what else to call it – makes room for us. For the Word of God which was *with God the Father from the beginning* (as the prologue to St John's Gospel so beautifully puts it) and through whom all things have their being, is made flesh (see John 1.3, 14). This is the flesh, God's word now made our flesh, that suffers all that being made flesh entails. We know that being human means being frail and mortal. We suffer. We die. God now knows this too.

However, we also believe that the same flesh that suffered on the cross, including the terrible anguish of abandonment, is now risen and ascended. Jesus really died on the cross and Jesus was really raised to life on the third day. Those who knew him in the flesh saw him. His resurrection was not the resuscitation of a corpse, nor some sort of ghostly apparition. The Gospel writers all make this plain. The new, resurrected life of Jesus is a raised-up and transformed physicality. Thomas touches him. Cleopas walks with him. Peter eats with him. He is the same person that died on the cross. But at the same time a new person, a new humanity, which is one of the reasons why he isn't immediately recognised. He bears the marks of his suffering.

Therefore, because God in Jesus has now experienced all that it is to be human *including the experience of alienation from God* and the utter despair that goes with it; and because in order for this to happen, and because God is Trinity, God the Father also experiences that estrangement from Jesus and the terrible loss that goes with it; then the whole life of God in Trinity is completely united with our life and therefore with all the frailties of our humanity. This means that when God raises Jesus from the dead, we – our humanity – are raised as well. What we see in the risen life of Jesus is nothing less than our own future, what the Bible calls the new creation.

On the cross, the Father and the Son are so deeply *separated* as to be apart. The experience of the passion is nothing less than the Godhead itself sharing in and experiencing the utter separation of humanity from God, which is our hopeless destiny without Christ's intervention.

On the cross, the Father and the Son are *one*, intimately united in the terrible abandonment that is the real price being paid for our salvation, our being united with God. When we talk about the cross as 'a price being paid', this is not a transaction, one person paying for something for someone else. The cross is for both Father and Son a single, surrendering moment as the work of salvation passes from activity, all the things that God had done in order to be known to us, to passion, God in Jesus surrendering to the last, inevitable trajectory of what it means to be a self-emptying God, whose nature and character is love, and who is reaching into the uttermost desolation of what it means to be separate from God, in order to bring us home.

'Whoever has seen me has seen the Father', says Jesus to Philip (John 14.9). This is true for all time and in all moments, which means that in Jesus' cry of abandonment we also see the Father's pain and anguish. The Father is not brokering a deal with the Son, nor exacting a debt as if the cross were a mere transaction. God is sounding the depths of our humanity and Jesus is choosing – electing – the way of undefended, abandoned love, even if it means feeling abandoned by God.

'In Christ God was reconciling the world to himself', writes Paul (2 Corinthians 5.19). 'He who did not withhold his own Son, but gave him up for all of us, will he not with him also give us everything else?' (Romans 8.32).

Both Father and Son suffer. Christ dies. And God the Father suffers the death of his beloved Son. As Jürgen Moltmann puts it: 'If the Son dies godforsaken on the cross, the Father also suffers the forsakenness of the Son.'[2]

He goes on in this beautiful passage:

> God goes with us, he suffers with us. Therefore, wherever Christ the Son of God goes, the Father goes with him. In the Son's sacrifice we can therefore also recognise the sacrifice of God; otherwise it would not be possible for the Gospel of John to say, 'Anyone who has seen me has seen the Father' (John 14.9). In the forsakenness of the Son, the Father also forsakes himself, he leaves his Heaven and is in Christ, in order to be the Father of all the forsaken on earth.[3]

The true cost of our salvation affects the whole Trinitarian life of God. And changes it, to the extent that our humanity is now carried into the life of the Godhead, that place prepared that

Jesus spoke of to his friends on the night before his crucifixion (see John 14.2).

If what happens on Calvary is more than the execution of Jesus in his humanity alone, it has significance for the whole Trinity, and therefore for us as well. Surely, it is the disclosure of God's total commitment to his world to choose the way of self-emptying and self-forgetful love, to be passive, and in the brutal face of all our rage and fury to be acted upon, to do nothing except forgive those who drive in the nails. To suffer and to die. To never threaten our freedom, never coerce or force us to respond, but to share what it is to be human. God shares our pain, our sorrow, our anger, our loneliness, our abandonment, even death itself. And in so doing, God redeems us, for now we are united with God. God's life is united with ours.

We do our very worst and God just keeps on loving us, not fighting back, not exacting revenge, not giving in to rage and hate in the ways we do, and even experiencing this great pain of abandonment. Within the life of God, both Father and Son feel equally forsaken, and we see what love looks like.

Indeed, isn't this the most painful and beautiful mystery of all, that in order to love one must suffer. That love always involves suffering. We may, of course, wish for the suffering to end, but so often our suffering is the consequence of our love. When someone dies, we grieve. That grief is painful and endless. We think we might be getting over it, and then it rises up to assault us afresh, as if the wound was only made yesterday. Therefore, we say God suffers with us and for us, not just in Jesus but in the whole life of God. And because God's nature is love, and because we know love suffers, then we have to conclude that God suffers as well because God is love.

'Only the suffering God can help', wrote Dietrich Bonhoeffer from his prison cell in the Flossenbürg concentration camp.[4]

Isn't this why we gather at the cross? Because on that cross we see the suffering love of a suffering God? And why in the liturgy of Good Friday we are taken beyond words and explanations simply to stand and look – and if we dare, hold and touch and kiss the wood of the cross with quiet thankfulness, remembering the weight it carried, which is us and our great pain and sorrow, but also the weight of care and love that God bears for the world.

And there is such wrong in the world. And such hurt.

As I was doing the final edit of this book, Russia invaded Ukraine. As I write, a nuclear power plant near Kyiv has been bombed. Unspeakable horrors are playing out before our eyes and what is worst in us struts across the world, oblivious to human suffering, impervious to mercy or persuasion, entirely consumed by the privileges of unchecked power, a terrible evil. Such wrong in our hearts, such potential for harm, such horrifying consequences for the world and for each of us in it.

We cannot save ourselves. That is the terrible human diagnosis. There is good in us. But there is also dreadful fallenness. God has had to come and do for us what we could never do for ourselves. And it cost a lot. But that is what love does. In Jesus, our true humanity is restored and revealed. We find our home with God. We are shown what our humanity can be. Amazingly, we are also seeing some of this at the moment in Ukraine: small acts of self-sacrificing kindness for those we love, and even trying, against the odds of what is worst in us, to love our enemies.

We stand at the cross with one another. We start to make the connections. It is still ghastly. We are looking at ourselves at our worst as Jesus is killed. But we are also looking at God in God's most astonishing and beautiful demonstration of unending and incomparable love. The stamp of the cross is not just at the heart of Jesus, but in the heart of God. The risen and ascended Christ bears the marks of the nails. Therefore, in these the most hopeless words of all, we find the greatest hope of all. That God in Jesus Christ really did share everything about our humanity. When this happens, we also find ourselves standing alongside that centurion who first glimpsed what this means and made his declaration of faith; and with the thief who hung alongside Jesus and asked to be remembered; and with Mary the mother of Jesus and that small band of tenacious women who unlike all the others kept faith and kept vigil through the long hours of his dying. With all of them, we arrive at a place of adoration and thanksgiving. For our devotion to the cross would be an unnatural and masochistic obsession were it not for the fact that God's pain and God's sorrow are united in God's love; a love that endures pain and death, forgives sins, restores lost unity.

These words of Jesus are the most bleak. They are also the most hopeful. As a child once put it in a prayer one Good Friday morning many years ago at the activity club we were running in the church I was serving in at the time: 'We now have a path to heaven. The cross is a signpost to life.'

~

I was a curate in South London. There was a Church of England Primary School in the parish and it was my happy duty to go into the school most weeks; sometimes to take an assembly (I think we call it collective worship nowadays); sometimes to be in a class; and sometimes even to lead some lessons. All this was certainly an education for me!

Wanting to teach the basics of the Christian faith, there was one occasion when I set about teaching a class of seven- and eight-year-olds the doctrine of the Trinity. Well, I was just a curate at the time, inexperienced and wet behind my clerical collar.

I conceived a four-session lesson plan. The first week I would talk about God the Father, the second, God the Son, and the third, God the Holy Spirit. In each of the lessons, I would talk about some of the traditional imagery and iconography associated with the three distinct – but united! – persons of the Trinity and get the children to draw pictures.

The first three lessons went really well. The children seemed to understand what I was saying and each week they produced some lovely pictures. God the Father tended to end up as an old man with a beard sitting on a cloud, even though I had stressed that God was neither male nor female and that heaven wasn't 'up there'. However, drawing something that is without source or origin and is uncreated is not an easy task. I spoke about God as creator, and the best pictures were of the creation itself, rather than the one who made it. But it seemed to go okay.

Jesus was easier. He is, after all, the human face of God, so there were lots of babies in mangers, good shepherds and rosy-cheeked images of Jesus smiling from the cross.

The Holy Spirit was the best of all. The powerful imagery of the Spirit is made for illustration. I had a classroom full of mighty winds, rushing waters, sizzling flames and descending doves. All was going swimmingly well.

Then came week four. The Trinity itself. On the evening before the final lesson it dawned on me – rather late in the day I must confess – that I had bitten off rather more than I could chew. I wanted, of course, to say to the children that though we know God has three persons, and that these persons are distinct, they are, nevertheless, one God and one unity of persons. But this is not an easy concept and as all Christians know, can only be understood through the person of Jesus, who shows us the Father and sends us the Spirit. It is hard to depict that in a single image. Triangles and three-leaved clover are the best the Christian imagination has managed to muster over the centuries, and although I realised I would have to share these images with the children, I wanted to offer them something myself. But what?

Better theological imaginations than mine have stumbled on this road, but late in the day, I came up with the idea of a dolls' house with the front taken off, the fire burning in the hearth and a crucifix over the mantelpiece. I drew my picture to show them the next day. I explained that it was one house, but it had three elements: it had been created, and that God the Father was a creator, and that within it there was a fire symbolising the presence of the Spirit spreading its warmth throughout the house, and the cross upon which Christ died was visible throughout (well, not quite).

Of course, this is heresy. In my depiction of the Trinity, the different parts of the house and the things within it can hardly be said to be equal. Nor does one in any way proceed from the other. Nor is there any real relationship between them except that the cross and the fire are inside the same house. But, as I say, it was late in the day. I couldn't think of anything else. I had to say something, and I hoped that the little bit of heresy in the picture could be made up for by my explanations.

Of course, I was wrong. I was expecting too much of them. I soldiered on anyway. There was always the triangle to fall back on.

I showed them my picture. I gave my explanation. I ended by saying that I was sure they could come up with better ideas than me. But, hardly surprisingly, they couldn't.

Except one little girl.

As I trudged round the classroom looking at one triangle after another, easily drawn and still twenty minutes of the lesson to go, or else at variations of my dolls' house, but with a Good Shepherd over the mantelpiece rather than a cross, I came across Jessie's drawing.

Jessie had drawn three trees in a field. The first was an apple tree, a symbol of creation. The second was a vine, because Jesus had said 'I am the true vine'. The third was a tree in autumn with the leaves being blown off by the wind. And under the ground, the roots of the three trees combined together.

It was an astonishing image. To this day, I wished I'd asked Jessie if I could have kept it, or at least made a copy of it. However, I can still see it in my head, and I am astounded at the ways in which she had pieced all this together and the profound theological imagination that she had brought to bear in the task. I couldn't even remember whether I had spoken about Jesus saying he was the true vine. I might have done. But somehow, Jessie had got there.

What was equally amazing was that although Jessie was a pupil at a Church of England Primary School where clergy went in every week and where there were, of course, Christian assemblies and daily prayer, she was not herself a member of the church and nor were her family. Contrary to some misinformed opinion, most Church of England schools are community schools serving everyone in their catchment area, and Jessie went to this school simply because it was her local school.

But she had made a connection. She had drawn something that made sense of the greatest and most important mystery at the heart of the Christian faith, that God is a community of persons and that in order to understand God we need to make this connection. Moreover, she had done it in one great imaginative leap of faith. Aged seven.

That's not quite the end of the story. Like many clergy, I kept a little list of people I encountered in the parish who were not yet part of the Christian community, and I was always on the lookout for an opportunity to visit them and encourage them into the life of the church.

The following week, I made a point of being at the school gate at the end of the day when children were being picked up and was therefore able to meet Jessie's mum and say to her what a beautiful picture Jessie had made in the lesson. We chatted, and I asked whether it would be okay to pop in sometime. Mum said yes, and one day after school, I did pop in, and unsurprisingly to me, but of great and unexpected intrigue and surprise to her parents, discovered that Jessie was asking them all sorts of questions about the Christian faith and had said to them that she would like to go to church.

But her parents had never been to church in their lives and didn't quite know where to begin. I said I could help them.

What a happy day it was a few months later when I baptised Jessie and her two sisters and her whole family were welcomed into the fellowship of faith.

Saint Cyprian described his own coming to faith as inhalation: 'one gulp by a sudden act of grace'.[5]

This, I suppose, or something like it, is what happened to the centurion standing at the foot of the cross when he declared Jesus to be the Son of God. He just got it. He probably wouldn't know how to explain it. However, he saw something in Jesus – in his dying – which enabled him to make all the connections; that this forsaken and abandoned man, who refused to fight back and forgave those who put him there, was God.

Jessie, too, made the connection. She simply understood who God is and wanted to be part of that community that followed God.

I don't know the real end of Jessie's story. I don't know what happened to her and how her faith has shaped her life or where it has led her, though I would love to know and harbour a secret hope that this book might somehow find its way into her hands. And I am as mystified as anyone as to why some people seem to receive the gift of faith in such astonishing ways, and others never seem to get it at all. I'm thinking again of James sitting at my kitchen table, saying, 'So what am I, then?' But there is, for all of us, a connection to be made, especially when we are feeling broken ourselves and facing pain and separation. And especially when we are seeking. When we make the decision to look for God. When we suspend all our disbelief for a moment (as we do every time we go to the theatre or the cinema) and live lives *as if* God is real and then find God *is* real. There is one who is with us. His roots have entwined with ours.

Questions

1. Share some stories of when you have made a connection and faith has become real, or when you have seen this happening to others.
2. What are the advantages and challenges of thinking about God suffering? Surely if God is all-powerful, God cannot suffer?
3. How does it change and help our understanding of the cross to think about it as something that affects the whole life of God, not just Jesus?
4. Share some stories about standing at the cross, or perhaps holding on to the cross (many Christians have a holding cross in their pocket or wear one round their neck). How has this helped you, particularly in times of grief or difficulty?

SEVEN

Jesus' howl of anguish from the cross is the cry of the human soul in all its suffering and the sign that our humanity in all its joy and sadness is taken into the life of God in the Trinity.

The letter to the Hebrews says that Jesus offered himself up to God 'through the eternal Spirit' (see Hebrews 9.14). The link between the Father and the Son in the death and agony and separation of the cross is the Holy Spirit.[1] The surrender of the Father and the offering of the Son take place through the Spirit. The cross, we discover, is not left behind; rather, it is relocated at the heart of God. In fact, we can even dare to say that something has changed in God. The God who cannot suffer chooses and elects to become the suffering one. This isn't just Jesus suffering in his humanity, but all of God – Father, Son and Holy Spirit – is immersed and engaged in the suffering of Jesus. And because the Risen Jesus bears the marks of suffering, then those marks, those glorious scars, are present for eternity in the heart and life of God.

The Risen Jesus appears in the locked-in room of the locked-in lives of the fearful and defeated disciples gathered in the upper room, scared witless that what has happened to Jesus might now happen to them. The first thing he does is show them his hands and his side. What he is showing them is the wounds of his suffering love. Then he says those words that themselves sum up all that God has achieved for us in Christ: 'Peace be with you' (John 20.19). This is the true and abiding peace, the *shalom*, a totality of well-being and restored community that is the peace of Christ, a peace that the world cannot give or ever truly understand. The cost of that love and of that peace are marked in Jesus' hands and feet, and in the wounded side, which Thomas is invited to touch. It is therefore an imprint in the life of God.

The cross is also at the heart of humanity, showing the best and the worst of us. It is the means by which we are saved; that is, the means by which our true life is restored to us and we have peace with God and the great hope of peace with one another – what the letter to the Ephesians refers to as us who 'once were far off' being 'brought near by the blood of Christ' (Ephesians 2.13). The letter goes on:

> For [Christ] is our peace; in his flesh he has . . . broken down the dividing wall, that is, the hostility between us. He has abolished the law with its commandments and ordinances, so that he might create in himself one new humanity . . . thus making peace.
>
> (EPHESIANS 2.14–15)

The letter speaks about two groups of people and is therefore speaking specifically about Jews and Gentiles. However, this extends to all the ways we are divided from each other, from God, and even from the earth itself. Therefore, it means there is no place for race hatred, prejudice, homophobia, misogyny, transphobia or xenophobia in a new humanity, which has been reconciled to Christ and therefore to each other. All are brought into reconciliation and community with God 'in one body through the cross' (Ephesians 2.16), thus putting to death that hostility by which we became separated in the first place. What was lost is restored.

Our life is joined to God's life by the cross. Jesus shares our dereliction, our suffering and our death, and by Christ's victory over sin (those things that nailed him to the cross) and separation, we are united in Christ as a new humanity with a message of hope for the world.

We are given a new identity – those who are reconciled. Quoting the prophet Hosea, the first letter of Peter says, 'Once you were not a people, but now you are God's people; once you had not received mercy, but now you have received mercy' (1 Peter 2.10).

So that is who we are: the people of God, called out of darkness into God's glorious light (see 1 Peter 2.9).

This letter of Peter is written to Christians in exile, experiencing suffering and persecution. It speaks to us in our exile and in our suffering. By his passion, death and resurrection, and by faith in Christ and through the waters of baptism, we are born into a living hope (see 1 Peter 1.3).

As we have discovered, the passion of Jesus Christ is nothing less than the passion of God in the Trinity. Thus we can acknowledge a contradiction in some Christian understanding that is, perhaps, at the heart of the atheist complaint about God, and at the heart of our own difficulty in justifying God when we face suffering ourselves, or when we cry out in anger and disbelief that there can be the sort of terrible suffering in the world that we see about us every day.

We say that God cannot suffer, and yet it is God who suffers on the cross. As we have seen, if we try and understand the cross only in terms of Christ's suffering, and at that only in his humanity, then not only are we failing to be true to our belief in the Trinity – or to the insights into the Trinitarian sharing of the passion that I have tried to elucidate here – but we make the cross callous and cruel, and not just the callous cruelty of our humanity, but of God. The cross can only be the source and sign of our salvation if it is also the ultimate declaration and embodying of God's self-giving love in Trinity.

'In Christ God was reconciling the world to himself', said the apostle Paul (2 Corinthians 5.19). However, God doesn't do this by a display of power, but with humility and love. When the letter to the Philippians says God 'emptied himself' (Philippians 2.7), it does not mean God stopped being powerful for a short while so as to become limited and human in Jesus, but that God's real and actual power was always the power of love. That love has been emptied into Jesus so that we could see it and receive it. And because it is love, God does not force himself upon us. Otherwise, it would be something other than love. God waits. God waits for the free response of our love to God's love. That is the other reason why Mary does not recognise Jesus in the garden, nor Cleopas and his companion on the Emmaus Road. It's not just that Jesus is alive with a new life. She must make the step of love, the connection of faith herself. As we must do.

In the passion of Christ and in his resurrection, we discover that the living God, the risen God, is the loving God. But can a God who does not suffer, really love? And can a God who does not love really be a God at all, certainly not a God worthy of worship and adoration, nor a God who can connect and teach us about ourselves, and give us the new identity we long for: as we have already acknowledged, we know love most in the suffering it brings. Such a God would either be irrelevant, or worse, a monster, albeit a hugely powerful one. And definitely one to appease and satisfy.

But the God who is in Jesus shows us something else. This God displays living and loving through sharing and through participating in our life, which includes our suffering. God even becomes vulnerable to our responses: takes the risk on Easter morning that Mary wouldn't recognise him; that Peter might go on denying him.

We have the same choices to make. Either God lets people suffer or God suffers as well; in and through the creation, and particularly and resolutely, through Christ. The God who merely lets the innocent suffer stands accused in our courts (and in the death of Jesus adds one more pointless death to all the others). But the God who through the cross of Christ suffers *everything* in *everyone* is God's only possible defending Council.

Therefore, when we find ourselves saying – as of course we do – where is God when this terrible tragedy happens, when a child dies, when an atrocity takes place, when Ukraine is invaded, when a virus attacks, when a slagheap slips onto a school, or a crazed gunman steps into a classroom, we must look no further than the cross. And this, as Moltmann also points out, is the question: not so much, 'why?' but 'where?' Where is God when this happens? We know it happens. And we know it will go on happening. And we will never really know why. But what of God? *Where* is God in all of this?

He is where we put him. It is where God chooses to be. He is on the cross. He is crying out again in our cries. When we discover this, says Moltmann, we will feel his presence in our suffering and discover 'the spring from which life can be born anew'.[2] That is, I suppose, the water and blood that flow from Christ's riven heart on the cross.

This is where we will always find God. It is the only way of demonstrating that in this world of sin and failure, frailty and death, God is with us, saving us, raising us up, pointing to that resurrection life that is prepared for us beyond death and showing us that despite all the horrible evidence to the contrary, and what appears to be the meaningless tragedy of life, 'Yea, though I walk through the valley of the shadow of death, I will fear no evil; for thou art with me, thy rod and thy staff comfort me.'[3]

Christ is risen. He has made the dead wood of the cross the promise of life for ever. Which doesn't mean pain and suffering have gone away. But it does mean they are changed. I'm thinking again now of Chris, who if you remember, as he was dying, didn't know what to pray for any more. Yet somehow, his resolute faithfulness, even when he had nothing left to say, sustained him in the valley of the shadow of death. So at his funeral, as someone who is also fearful, and someone who also often doesn't know what to pray, and whose faith feels fragile, and who writes these books to persuade and convert himself again as much as anyone else, I could declare with St Paul: 'Where, O death, is your victory? Where, O death, is your sting?' (1 Corinthians 15.55).

Like Paul, and in the teeth of suffering and often overwhelmed by despair, and often feeling as if I'm in the dark, or sinking beneath the waves, I have come to say that I too 'am convinced that neither death, nor life, nor angels, nor rulers, nor things present, nor things to come, nor powers, nor height, nor depth, nor anything else in all creation, will be able to separate us from the love of God in Christ Jesus our Lord' (Romans 8.38–9).

For Mark, whose Gospel account we have been sticking with throughout this book, this connection, and the hope it signifies, is illustrated by the tearing of the curtain in the temple from top to bottom. Significantly, this happens just as Jesus dies, just after he has uttered his cry of terrifying abandonment, and just before the centurion makes his announcement. So the account reads:

> When it was noon, darkness came over the whole land until three in the afternoon. At three o'clock Jesus cried out with a loud voice, 'Eloi, Eloi, lema sabachthani?' which means, 'My God, my God, why have you forsaken me?' When some of the bystanders heard it, they said, 'Listen, he is calling for Elijah.' And someone ran, filled a sponge with sour wine, put it on a stick, and gave it to him to drink, saying, 'Wait, let us see whether Elijah will come to take him down.' Then Jesus gave a loud cry and breathed his last. And the curtain of the temple was torn in two, from top to bottom. Now when the centurion, who stood facing him, saw that in this way he breathed his last, he said, 'Truly this man was God's Son!'
>
> (MARK 15.33–9)

The curtain in the temple takes a bit of understanding. Mark is probably referring to the curtain that separated the holiest place in the temple from everything else, the place where the high priest would go each year on the Day of Atonement. The rending of this veil speaks powerfully of all the barriers between

God and the world being broken down through Jesus' death on the cross. There is now access to God in ways that have not been available before. Indeed, even the need for a temple and a high priest are called into question.

The prophet Isaiah cried out, 'O that you would tear open the heavens and come down, so that the mountains would quake at your presence' (Isaiah 64.1). The tearing of the curtain is also the tearing down of the barriers between earth and heaven, which is why in Matthew's Gospel at this precise point we are also told, 'The earth shook, and the rocks were split' (Matthew 27.51). He is emphasising the point. Something of cataclysmic importance has happened.

These ideas are taken up and developed in the letter to the Hebrews. We are told that we have 'confidence to enter the sanctuary', that is into the presence of God, the presence that was beyond us, 'by the blood of Jesus, by the new and living way that he opened for us *through the curtain* (that is, through his flesh)' (Hebrews 10.19–20, my italics). In other words, the tearing and breaking of his flesh is the means by which we recover union with God. The tearing of the curtain in the temple shows that we don't need temples any more. In Christ, we have direct access to God.

Earlier in the letter, in a beautiful image, this hope is described as 'a sure and steadfast anchor of the soul, a hope that enters the inner shrine behind the curtain, where Jesus, a forerunner on our behalf, has entered, having become a high priest for ever according to the order of Melchizedek' (Hebrews 6.19–20).

Jesus has become our High Priest. The sacrificial offering he brings is himself.

He has become the temple, the place where we worship and in whom we have access to God. This is why John says in the Book of Revelation that 'I saw no temple in the city, for its temple is the Lord God the Almighty and the Lamb' (Revelation 21.22).

In the words of the great theologian Jürgen Moltmann, 'In

the midst of the unbearable story of the passion of the world we can discover the reconciling story of the passion of Christ.'

~

I became the ninety-eighth Archbishop of York in July 2020, during the first lockdown, which was the means by which we protected one another from the worldwide Covid pandemic that fixed the whole world in a fearful paralysis throughout that year and through all of 2021. As I write, we are learning to live with COVID-19, but it has not gone away. Across the world, millions of people have suffered.

All of us have learned how to live differently. Perversely and inevitably, the poorest have suffered the most. Vaccines are available for the wealthy, but not so much for the poor. Nevertheless, we are all more acutely aware of our frailty and mortality than has been the case for a long time. This may yet lead to some sort of spiritual revival in the wealthy countries of the West who have for so long felt immune to the ravages of plague and illness, which were the commonplace reality for most human beings through most of history.

Furthermore, in Europe, most of us have enjoyed almost unbroken peace for the whole of our lives. Some people can still remember the Second World War. Most of us can't. Hitler was defeated. We saw the Cold War thaw. We truly believed that peace was the new normal for the human race in Europe.

Russia's invasion of Ukraine has shattered that illusion, or at least reminded us that peace cannot be taken for granted. Our neglect of those international associations and bonds of well-being will have their consequences if we allow walls of separation to be built between nations. The message of the cross of Christ and its breaking down of barriers is a call today for nations to live in peace and for us to build all our social policies upon the fundamental truth of our humanity, which is that we belong to each other, one humanity inhabiting one world. Little England on its own will not flourish. We must love our neighbour and rebuild community in Europe. In this way, and in this way only, will we find peace.

Because I became archbishop during the lockdown it meant that when I moved from being Bishop of Chelmsford, a wonderfully moving chapter in my life where I had had the privilege of serving the diocese in which I grew up and where I had a deep sense of belonging, there was no opportunity for a farewell service. I said goodbye to the diocese I had served for ten years by simply waking up one day and having to acknowledge that this bit of my life was gone.

As it happened, that day was Easter Day. I couldn't sleep. The night before, Rebecca (my wife) and I had lit a fire in the garden, and kindled an Easter flame from the fire, performing our own little homemade version of the great liturgy of Easter. These were the days when churches were closed; we were isolated from each other, only allowed out for essential shopping and one walk a day, and learning how to inhabit life differently.

So I got up in the very early hours of the morning, sat by the embers of the fire, poked them back to life and contemplated the move from Chelmsford to York.

Because it was the very early days of lockdown, we hadn't even learned how to do Zoom conferences very well, so the actual goodbye to Chelmsford was done via a little film that was posted on Facebook. In it, I am given a picture. It is a large print by the Scottish painter Craigie Aitchison. I'm standing and looking at it as I write these words.

In the picture, a simple, forlorn and forsaken Christ is alone on the cross. There is virtually nothing else in the painting. The cross stands in an empty, though vivid and brightly coloured landscape. Behind the cross and in the distance two animals, possibly two sheep, maybe one dog chasing a sheep, scutter across the horizon.

Craigie Aitchison painted an image like this over and over again, literally hundreds of times. Some of them are small, intimate paintings and drawings. Some are large prints like mine. Some are stained-glass windows, like the ones you can see in Liverpool Cathedral or the very large window in St Mary The Boltons in West London. The picture on the front cover of this book is a photograph of that window.

In some of the paintings, like this one, there is a dog sitting at the foot of the cross. Nevertheless, in all the pictures, Christ is alone, insofar as there are no other people.

Christ is abandoned. Forsaken. Godforsaken.

I've always found these images profoundly moving. They are both contemplative – just Christ upon the cross, the cross fixed into the landscape of the world – and disturbing: the utter loneliness of the cross. Christ's abandonment. Everyone has fled.

And if we look at the picture and recite those awful words, *Eloi, Eloi*, then we sense that this abandonment is also, for Christ, in these final moments of his earthly life, the departure of God.

It is said that Craigie Aitchison's lifelong fascination with the cross was triggered by a visit to see Salvador Dalí's famous *Christ of Saint John of the Cross* – the one where the cross hovers over the world and Christ looks down on the world from the cross. My parents gave me a copy of that picture on the day I was confirmed. But the hopeful, magical, soaring image of Dalí can hardly be found in Craigie Aitchison's lonely and isolated images of Christ. Christ is leaving the world and the world has left him.

I am enormously grateful to the people and parishes of the Chelmsford diocese for their generosity and thoughtfulness in giving me this print. I spend a long time looking at it, and it has been behind all the things I've written in this book. It has also shaped the way I have navigated my way through the successive lockdowns of Covid. For although it does depict a forlorn and forsaken Christ, it is *still Christ*. He is *still present*. He is where we put him. He is where God chooses to be.

He endures.

He goes on suffering.

He goes on abiding.

He goes on loving.

Nothing gets in the way of the love of God that is in Christ Jesus, even in these terrifying moments of utter abandonment and forsakenness.

Moreover, my experience, and the experience of every Christian person during these months and years of lockdown, has been one of forsakenness. The things we took for granted and the things we relied on were taken away. They had to be. It was the way we protected and defended each other. But it was hard.

For Christian people, it even meant not being able to go to church, and therefore not receiving the sacraments that are the heartbeat and – quite literally – the lifeblood of our Christian life. I was fortunate, as a priest and a bishop, and as someone with a chapel in my house, I could go on presiding at the Eucharist and go on receiving Holy Communion, and I did my best, when I offered those services and received that communion, to do it, insofar as I was able, on behalf of all the people I served and all those who were having to fast from fellowship and from communion.

In this exile and in this fast, everything that we depended on to sustain our Christian life had to be suspended, but Christ remained. This was the paradox and the beauty of what happened to many people in the Church during lockdown. In losing our life, by which I mean the life of our usual disciple-ship, we found a new intimacy with Christ. Of course, this wasn't true for everyone, and I dread to think what it was like for many thousands of people, especially the poorest in our society and across the world, who not only didn't have a chapel in their house, but didn't have much space at all, and certainly didn't have a garden to sit in as I did. But, nevertheless, in so many conversations I have had since lockdown eased, I have discovered ordinary Christian people, often living out their Christian life in the most difficult of circumstances, saying that despite the difficulties and privations of the lockdown, and the terrible suffering that they had experienced, including the death of loved ones, and the unspeakable sadness of funerals where relatives couldn't even hold each other, or attend, they had experienced a new intimacy with Christ. They had found him again present and reaching out to them, alongside and inside their suffering, in the heart of a locked-down, separated and isolated world.

There we were, on our own, cut off in the upper rooms of our homes and unable to go to church, and Christ found us.

I see this in Craigie Aitchison's images of the isolated Christ, who is also the Christ who comes to us in isolation, helping us to know that we don't actually need anything else, and that in the end all the things we enjoy – material blessings, other people, the worship and comfort of the Church, the sacraments themselves – all of them will cease. All of them will have to be relinquished. There will be only Christ. He is the one in whom we will find our truest identity as those who are made in the image of God, redeemed and restored by Christ, finding ourselves within the life of the God who now bears the scars of passion.

We know this, because we know that our lives will end in death and that will be a parting from everything. We think of Lent as a time to give things up. But we often forget *why* we are giving them up. It is not to lose weight. It is not because God likes us better if we're a bit miserable. It's because one day we will have to give up everything. Even breathing itself. This is the journey we are on. This is the journey Christ shares with us. It is the story of that journey and the hope it brings that lies behind all the other little stories and reminiscences I have been sharing in this book.

We know that in death we find Christ, because we know that Christ has found us. He has met us at the precise point of our deepest need and our most extreme isolation, which is our death. This is the great story of the Christian faith. We know that he cried out in desperate loneliness, feeling utterly forsaken by God. And we know that this howl of anguish, which resonates with the cry of our hearts, was not the end, but the means by which the end was turned to a beginning. The veil of the temple was torn in two. The centurion standing there made the connection. The dead body of Christ, laid in the tomb, was raised to life.

So now this picture hangs in my study. I look at it every day and pray that I can be a person who comes to the foot of the cross, who inhabits these empty spaces where I see Christ forsaken, and can become someone who does this in the world around me and in all the communities I serve, where there is so much lostness and sadness and forsakenness. I pray that we may be a church that can do the same, which is why, as I have tried to lead the Church of England in discerning what God might be saying to us at this time, we have come up with the simple phrase that we believe God is calling us to be a Christ-centred Church.

On the one hand, this is the most obvious thing to say about the Church of Jesus Christ – what are we if we are not a people centred on Christ?

On the other, it is the most profound, for we are endlessly called to come back to the cross of Christ, to stand under it and to understand it.

Which is why this picture helps me, and why although in my picture there is no dog sitting at the foot of the cross, I find myself often thinking about those faithful dogs seen in so many of Craigie Aitchison's other crucifixions.

I started out thinking, how strange, *even* dogs come to the cross. Then I thought, how amazing, *only* dogs come to the cross.

Maybe it's the same dogs that the feisty Syro-Phoenician woman told Jesus ate the crumbs that fell from the Master's table (see Mark 7.24–30). But I don't see it quite like that.

I see the dog sitting at the foot of the cross as an image of obedient faithfulness. Standing firm, offering steadfast dependability, even when understanding falls short.

I do believe you need to stand under the cross to understand it. However, I also know that understanding will always be elusive, because God comes to us in human flesh. What he makes for us here is a relationship with God, and relationships only work when you enter into them. And you will never understand completely. Mostly, because there is always more to know.

Questions

1. Look at the picture on the front of this book. What does it say to you? What do you make of the dog sitting there?
2. What has been your experience of trying to live and sustain the Christian life in lockdown and in isolation? What have you learned? How has your faith changed?
3. Think about the soldier standing at the foot of the cross and what he said. As you stand at the foot of the cross, what do you want to say *to* Jesus or *about* Jesus?
4. Think of the curtain being torn in two. What barriers and separations are you aware of in your life, in your community and in the world? What do you think God wants to tear down? How might we be part of that?

AFTERWORD

We refer to the events that begin at the Last Supper and run through Gethsemane, Jesus' arrest and trial, his scourging before Pilate, his crucifixion, and his body being taken down from the cross and laid in the tomb as *his passion*. The biblical account is known as *the passion narrative*. This word, passion, is central to our understanding of these events. But what does the word passion mean?

The dictionary defines passion as a 'strong and barely controllable emotion'; an 'intense desire or enthusiasm for something'. Nowadays, we usually associate the word with intense sexual desire. To feel passionate towards someone is to feel a strong and insatiable yearning.

The root of the English word passion comes from the Latin *pati*, which means 'to suffer'. This gives us a second understanding of the word and the reason the narrative of the cross is described as a passion. It is the story of Christ's suffering.

The Greek word for suffer is similar. It is *pascho*. It has a slightly more nuanced meaning, not only referring to physical suffering but also carrying the sense of 'enduring', of being 'acted upon', what we might refer to as 'being passive'.

All three meanings are essential for our understanding of the cross.

The story of the cross is the story of God's passion and love for us; the love that God demonstrates in the life, death and resurrection of his Son. The Christian faith is God's love song. The lover delights to woo and win back the lost beloved, which is us, frail and forsaken humanity, estranged from God's love and desolate. So God's reconciling love is poured out for us; a love that plumbs the depths of our separation from God; hence, when Jesus cries out on the cross, 'My God, my God, why have you abandoned me?', we find that it is God's very self that is in Christ searching out the depths of our own experience of estrangement from God, even as the ancient passion plays put it, harrowing hell itself.

On the cross, Jesus makes this love his own. He draws upon the Psalms to comfort and equip him as he dies. Using the words of Psalm 31, Jesus places himself in God's hands (Psalm 31.5 and Luke 23.46). His anguished shout of forsakenness is from Psalm 22. And even in his crying out in thirst I hear the echo of another psalm: the opening verse of Psalm 63: 'Oh God, you are my God, I seek you, my soul thirst for you; my flesh faints for you, as in a dry and weary land where there is no water.' Such is God's passionate love.

But the death of Jesus is also a wicked execution. Crucifixion was a sophisticated, cruel and humiliating way of killing people. Perfected over many years so as to control and extend the duration of the death, thousands and thousands of people were killed in this unimaginably painful way. The fact that Jesus died after three hours is something of a mercy. Sometimes people could be on the cross for days before death took them. That's why the soldiers were surprised when they came and found Jesus was already dead. The passion of Jesus is therefore the suffering of Jesus, and there is no avoiding it. Not only does Jesus share our death, he also shares and participates in a most dismaying and ignominious death.

Third, in his arrest and trial and flogging and execution, Jesus' whole ministry passes from being active to *being passive*.

Up until his arrest, Jesus commands attention by his purposeful words and actions. He may be enigmatic about who he is, wanting people to follow him and not just follow his teaching, and not just follow because they've been charmed by his miraculous works. He is emphatic about why he has come and what he must do. 'The kingdom of God has come near', he says (Mark 1.15).

Reading from the prophet Isaiah in the synagogue at Nazareth, and deliberately finding the place where it is written: 'The Spirit of the Lord is upon me, because he has anointed me to bring good news to the poor. He has sent me to proclaim release to the captives and recovery of sight to the blind, to let the oppressed go free, to proclaim the year of the Lord's favour', Jesus says that 'today this scripture has been fulfilled in your hearing' (Luke 4.18–19, 21).

Jesus couldn't be plainer or more provocative. He has come as a sign and fulfilment of God's presence and God's purposes. Those who follow him must also pursue this agenda.

Jesus embodies this kingdom *in himself*, not just by his words and actions. No wonder his followers were so shocked when, at his arrest, and when he had the opportunity to prove his identity, he changes from being the *one who acts* to becoming the one *who is acted upon*. In this respect, those terrible words of abandonment from the cross are the words of one who has completely abandoned himself to his fate, who allows those who have arrested him to do their worst. He is silent before his accusers. He is whipped and beaten. He does not retaliate. He even speaks words of peaceful and generous forgiveness to those who nail his hands and feet to the wood and crown him, a puppet king in their estimation, with twisted thorn.

This is not what we expect. It is not what we like. However, it is the divine method. Jesus defeats sin and death by the power of enduring love. When we do our worst, he gives his best. Our worst is sin and spite and rage and envy and greed, the very things that separate us from God and from each other, the very things that fuel the horrors of the world. And God's best is love, the revelation of God's very self: the love that turns the other cheek; the love that walks the second mile; the love that keeps no record of wrongs; the love that carries on doing what love must carry on doing, which is to go on loving.

As a sign of this love to his, as yet, uncomprehending friends and disciples, before his passion; before the demonstration of his yearning love; before his participation in the physical suffering of death; before his handing himself over to be acted upon; he does one last thing; one last action. In a simple act of far-reaching and powerful humility, he shows us what love looks like. He washes his disciples' feet. When we remember and re-enact the passion of Jesus, we do the same.

That is why we can turn to this story for hope. It is why we can find particular hope – even in these most unlikely of words – for when we do not know what to say or what to pray, like Jesus turning to the Psalms, we can mine that rich seam of poetry, petition and praise within the Bible itself, and this will lift you, and hold you, and give you a voice. Because prayer, at its most basic, is longing for God and crying out to God, even in utter dejection and desperation.

For isn't it the case that we, too, often feel abandoned by God? We turn to God, but we can't always find him. In the small hours of the night when the chill fears of death grip our hearts, or when we find ourselves torn away from those we love, or when so many questions rise and churn in our minds, and the universe in all its vast and amazing beauty feels bereft of meaning or hope, we feel impossibly small and insignificant, and God feels absent. In these dark moments, do we not cry out to the God we hardly believe in: My God, why have you abandoned me?

In these moments, we can find comfort knowing Jesus cried out too. We can find comfort in the psalms that articulate horror and regret as well as praise. We can remember that *wanting* to pray, *is* praying.

'My soul is athirst for God', says Psalm 42, 'even for the living God' (Psalm 42.2; *Common Worship* Psalter). Here is the link between prayer, the passion and the Psalms: Jesus cried out for me.

Similarly, on Easter Day we are invited to affirm again the promises of our baptism. If you do this, you will notice that you're not asked to express your certainty about things you undeniably know, but your sorrow about what has gone wrong and fallen short in your life, and your belief and trust in a person, Jesus, through who you have entered into community with God. It is in this relationship, which Jesus makes possible by his dying and rising, that we find our true identity and belonging. Hence, the symbolism and meaning of baptism is as much drowning as washing. We go down with Jesus into the dark waters of death. We are raised up with him to new life.

Thus it is that we come to the cross, thankful, expectant and obedient. Christ is there for us.

Moreover, all this is there for us, beyond words and on the other side of comprehension, in the actions of the liturgy of Holy Week.

On Palm Sunday, we wave our branches and sing Hosanna.

On Maundy Thursday, our feet are washed and we remember the gift of the Eucharist, which is itself the means by which we receive and celebrate the fruits of Christ's passion and death, how it is made real for us until that day when we see him face to face.

On Good Friday, we cry out, 'Crucify'. We are invited to stand at the cross. We can even step forward and touch the cross. Or hold the cross. Or kiss the cross.

In fact, one of my most precious memories of all the Good Friday liturgies I've attended is of a faithful elderly parishioner called Maud, to whom I used to take Holy Communion every week when I was a curate. I mentioned her earlier. She rarely managed to get to church, but there was one Good Friday when she was there. She was very, very frail. But she was determined to venerate the cross. It took her an age to come forward. But when she stood before the cross, a beautiful little lady bent over with the pain and depletion of age, and somehow managed to get to her knees and hold on to the cross and plant a kiss at the very point where Jesus' feet would have been nailed, I saw in her a radiance that told me Paul knew what he was talking about when he said that we, with our unveiled faces, will reflect the glory we see and be transformed by it (see 2 Corinthians 3.18). It was reflected in her suffering. It issued forth in devotion.

Maybe we thought that Paul was only talking about the glory of Christ's risen life. Well it is that, of course. But it is also the glory of the cross, Christ present with us in our suffering.

Finally, we come to the tomb in the night or very early on Sunday morning before dawn, and hear Jesus call our name. We renew the promises of our baptism, and hear him asking why we are weeping and whom we are seeking. We tell him the stories of our sorrow and desire.

He is the one we are looking for.

He is the one we have always been looking for, even when we did not know who he is. For he is the one who shows us what is best in us, our truest humanity and the fullness of life. His death and resurrection are the greatest hope of all.

Then we are sent out. We, too, the forsaken. We, the ones who have been gloriously found. We are sent out to seek and serve him in others and do the things he showed us. By this love, we will be known as his followers.

So let me finish with a story. It is a story I have told countless times. I don't know where it comes from, and I don't know whether it is true, but it sums up for me the reason Jesus cries out and the solace and the beauty we can find by standing with him under the cross.

It is about a little girl who is late to come home from school one day. Five minutes go by. Ten minutes go by. Her mother is worried sick. The little girl should have been home by now. Fifteen minutes go by. Twenty minutes go by. The mother anxiously paces up and down, fearing something terrible has happened. Twenty-five minutes go by, and just as the mother is on the verge of phoning the police, the little girl waltzes in through the back door, right as rain.

The mother sweeps her up in her arms, so relieved she is safe. But as is the way with us parents, relief quickly turns to anger: 'Where have you been?' says the mother. 'Didn't you know how worried I would be?'

'Well,' says the little girl, 'I was coming home from school, and I passed a woman carrying an enormous, beautiful vase. As I passed her, she tripped on a paving stone. The vase fell from her hands and broke into a thousand pieces.'

'Oh,' says the mother, 'is that why you're late? Did you stop to help her pick up the pieces?'

'No,' replies the little girl, 'I stopped to help her cry.'

The greatest hope

Two tragedies.

                       Untimely before your time
dying, like those whose names are writ in water;
and stoic slow demise, the spluttering wick
exhausting finite wax;

                    and one romantic fiction.
Boy meets girl, and children, always children,
play on endless loop and constitute
the vital repetitions of history.

Then one romantic fact.

                       Also young and
vital. Cast outside the city walls where
Sheol's replenishing waste chokes and smoulders,
where everyone ends up forsaken.
Puts a marker in the ground and says, no more,
so those who weep and wait and do not cling
may have something to hold on to.

There were times when I wanted to look away from the cross, but I dared not.

Julian of Norwich[1]

ACKNOWLEDGEMENTS

Like preaching, writing doesn't exist in a vacuum. It needs an audience. A book, or indeed a sermon, may appear to be a monologue, but really it's a conversation. It is shaped by the needs, aspirations, questions and longings of those to whom it is addressed.

Therefore, I am grateful for the congregations I have served over the years and the many people who have found my books helpful and whose input and encouragement has shaped them. Since this is a book that dares to look at some of life's hardest and darkest experiences, I want to acknowledge the blessings I have received from the people I have had the privilege of ministering to, particularly in difficult and painful circumstances. Some of them are named in the stories I tell. Most aren't. But I remember them in my heart and I'm thankful for their witness.

As I mentioned in the Introduction, this book began life as a series of Good Friday meditations preached in St Wilfrid's, Chichester, over thirty years ago. I then reworked these ideas in some Holy Week addresses in Chelmsford Cathedral in 2019, and then again, in the slipstream of the Covid pandemic, in York Minster in 2022. The commitment of these congregations to gather around the cross on Good Friday was my chief motivation for yet again coming and standing there myself and trying to be attentive to what I saw and heard. Therefore, many people's insights and observations are woven into this book, even if I have not been able to give specific acknowledgement in the text. We stand under the cross together. We learn together.

I am particularly grateful to my colleague Paul Ferguson, the Bishop of Whitby. Among his many gifts, he is a linguist. He had a close look at Chapter One for me, both to check I wasn't getting anything wildly wrong, and to make some helpful comments, which have improved the text. Nevertheless, any mistakes there, or anywhere else in the book for that matter, are entirely down to me.

The central idea of this book, that the cross reveals the deepest truth about God's passionate involvement with the world he loves, is shaped and inspired by the writing of Jürgen Moltmann, particularly in his books *The Crucified God* and *The Trinity and the Kingdom of God*, as well as some other papers he has written. Though as he acknowledges, wrestling with the idea of a God who suffers, and this as a powerful revelation of love, is a particularly English phenomena. But I'm humbled to add what I hope is an accessible footnote to the scholarship and faithfulness of others who have helped me.

I've not always been able to properly reference some of the things I have learned and received from others, particularly Moltmann. Some parts of this book have been written and rewritten over many years and I've simply lost track of where – in a few places – other people's words have become my words, and those places where other people's words remain but I haven't been able to track down where they came from. I apologise.

I've also set up the book as a kind of dialogue between the theological journey of digging deeply into these words chapter by chapter, and the stories and reminiscences from my ministry as a priest and a bishop that are placed alongside them. There isn't any particular logic to these second halves of each of the chapters; they are just the stories that resonate for me with the ideas of the chapter and therefore, hopefully, build a picture of how different things make sense to us when we stand under the cross. So there is a linear argument running through the book – we are taken from A to B as we work out what these words mean. And a circular one – we walk round the cross, seeing it from different angles and allow different parts of it to echo in our hearts and with different bits of our lives.

I'm also indebted to the writers of many other books about the cross and passion of Christ, those who have painted pictures or written poems about the crucifixion, and those who have set Jesus' words from the cross to music. Some of these do get a formal acknowledgement in the text. Many don't. This is simply because their music, words and images have got inside me and become part of me. That's what happens when we stand at the cross in the company of others.

Finally, I wish to thank my colleagues at Bishopthorpe for their patience with an archbishop who persists in writing books, and Katherine Venn, Nick Fawcett, Jessica Lacey and the team at Hodder for their encouragement and their various improvements to the text. In the end, the publication of any book is the work of a team.

Stephen Cottrell
Holy Week 2022

NOTES

Epigraph

1 Try as I might, I have simply been unable to track down the source of this quotation.

Introduction

1 Many biblical commentators think Paul, who wrote this letter, may be quoting from an already well-known hymn or prayer. Since Philippians was written in about AD 61, this means that the hymn/prayer itself would have been written very shortly after the death and resurrection of Christ.

2 I have written about this way of looking at the cross in my book, *I Thirst: The Cross – The Great Triumph of Love*, Hodder & Stoughton, 2003.

3 *Common Worship, Daily Prayer*, Church House Publishing, 2005, p. 250.

Chapter One

1 Matthew 5.1–12.

2 C. S. Lewis famously identified four: *philia* (friendship), *eros* (sexual), *storgé* (familial affection) and *agapé* (altruistic spiritual love). Neither *eros* nor *storgé* appear in the New Testament.

Chapter Two

1 The Hebrew original is '*Lamah lamah eli 'azavtani*' (the ' denotes a hard glottal stop). The Hebrew root '*zv* is the common word for 'leave' or 'forsake' and in various forms appears many times in the Old Testament.

2 Translations of this and other Psalms here are from the *Common Worship* Psalter.

3 William Shakespeare, *Hamlet*, Complete Works, Oxford University Press, 1905, p. 900.

4 Alfred, Lord Tennyson, 'Crossing the Bar', https://www.poetryfoundation.org/poems/45321/crossing-the-bar (accessed 1 January 2022).

5 William Shakespeare, *Henry VIII*, Complete Works, Oxford University Press, 1905, p. 650.

6 'Swing Low, Sweet Chariot' is the African American spiritual that English Rugby Union fans sing at matches.

7 Thomas Merton, *Praying the Psalms*, The Liturgical Press, 1956, p. 7.

8 V.5.

9 Dietrich Bonhoeffer, *The Psalms, Prayer Book of the Bible*, trans. Sister Isabel Mary, SLG Press, 1982, p. 8.

Chapter Three

1 The Order for the Celebration of Holy Communion, *Common Worship, Services and Prayers for the Church of England*, Church House Publishing, 2000, p. 173.

2 *Soul Music*, https://www.bbc.co.uk/programmes/b008mj7p.

3 I'm not sure who said this first, but I heard it from Bishop Michael Marshall in a sermon.

4 William Temple, *Nature, Man and God*, MacMillan and Co., 1949.

5 George Herbert, *Prayer (I)*, in *George Herbert, The Country*

Parson, The Temple, ed. with an Introduction by John Wall Jr, SPCK, 1981, p. 167.

Chapter Five

1 Philip Larkin, 'Aubade', in *Collected Poems*, Faber and Faber, 1988, p. 208.
2 Ibid.
3 *Common Worship, Services and Prayers for the Church of England*, Church House Publishing, 2000, p. 173.
4 Philip Larkin, 'Aubade', in *Collected Poems*, Faber and Faber, 1988, p. 208.
5 Anne Testar, *Francis Bacon, Man and Beast*, Royal Academy of Arts, 2021, p. 67.
6 Ibid.
7 Rachel Mann, *Spectres of God*, Darton, Longman and Todd, 2021, p. 52.
8 Mann, ibid., p. 51.

Chapter Six

1 The Apostles' Creed, in the version found in *The Book of Common Prayer*. Luther wrote that, 'Not only in the eyes of the world and his disciples, nay, in his own eyes too did Christ see himself as lost, as forsaken by God, felt in his own conscience that he was cursed by God, suffered the torments of the damned, who feel God's eternal wrath, shrink back from it and flee.' Quoted in Jürgen Moltmann, *The Trinity and the Kingdom of God: The Doctrine of God*, SCM Press Ltd, 1980, p. 77.
2 Jürgen Moltmann, 'The Passion of Christ and the Suffering of God', *The Asbury Theological Journal*, Vol. 48, No. 1 (spring 1993), p. 23.
3 Moltmann, ibid., p. 24.

4 Dietrich Bonhoeffer, *Letters and Papers from Prison*, Macmillan Publishing Company, 1972.

5 Cyprian, *Letter to Donatus*, in *Celebrating the Saints, Daily Spiritual Readings for the Calendar of the Church of England*, Canterbury Press, 1998, p. 319.

Chapter Seven

1 This is one of the central ideas of Jürgen Moltmann's thesis about how the passion of Christ can only really be understood by reference to the Trinity. These arguments find their fullest form in his book *The Trinity and the Kingdom of God: The Doctrine of God*, SCM Press Ltd, 1980.

2 Jürgen Moltmann, 'The Passion of Christ and the Suffering of God', *The Asbury Theological Journal*, Vol. 48, No. 1 (spring 1993), p. 27.

3 Psalm 23.4 in the version you will find in *The Book of Common Prayer*, one of the few psalms that some people may still know by heart.

Endmatter

1 Julian of Norwich, *Revelations of Divine Love*, trans. Clifton Wolters, Penguin Books, 1966, p. 92.